CW01086401

SOLZHENITSYN

SOLZHENITSYN

THE HISTORICAL-SPIRITUAL
DESTINIES OF RUSSIA AND THE WEST

LEE CONGDON

NIU Press / D e K a l b, I L

Northern Illinois University Press, DeKalb 60115
© 2017 by Northern Illinois University Press

26 25 24 23 22 21 20 19 18 17   1 2 3 4 5
978-0-87580-765-2 (paper)
978-1-60909-224-5 (e-book)
Book and cover design by Yuni Dorr

Library of Congress Cataloging-in-Publication Data
Names: Congdon, Lee, 1939– author.
Title: Solzhenitsyn : the historical-spiritual destinies of Russia and the
    West / Lee Congdon.
Description: DeKalb, IL : Northern Illinois University Press, 2017. |
    Includes bibliographical references and index.
Identifiers: LCCN 2017018637 (print) | LCCN 2017031143 (ebook) | ISBN
    9781609092245 (ebook) | ISBN 9780875807652 (cloth : alk. paper)
Subjects: LCSH: Solzhenitsyn, Aleksandr Isaevich, 1918–2008—Political
    and social views. | East and West.
Classification: LCC PG3488.O4 (ebook) | LCC PG3488.O4 Z6225 2017
    (print) | DDC 891.73/44—dc23
LC record available at https://lccn.loc.gov/2017018637

TO THEODORE LEACH AND DAVID BOVENIZER.

WITHOUT GOD . . . EVERYTHING IS PERMITTED.
—FYODOR DOSTOEVSKY

MEN HAVE FORGOTTEN GOD; THAT'S WHY ALL THIS HAS HAPPENED.
—ALEKSANDR SOLZHENITSYN

Contents

PREFACE

This is a study of Aleksandr Solzhenitsyn and his voluminous writings, particularly his reflections on the historical-spiritual destinies of Russia and the West—understood as distinct civilizations. It is not a biography of Solzhenitsyn, much less a history of modern Russia. It presents a straightforward argument—namely that Solzhenitsyn's warning to the West, that it had set out on a road similar to that which had led his own country into the abyss, should have been heeded. In that sense it offers a cultural critique—one based upon the historical record. In my judgment the "Slavophiles," opponents of the "Westernizers," who wished to remake Russia in the image of the West, were right to reject the Western model of development and to insist that Russia retain its own identity; for them, Moscow, not St. Petersburg, Peter the Great's "Window on the West," was the real Russia.

There are many reasons for Russia's singular character, including the legacy of the Mongol period (1240–1480), which meant, among other things, that Russia never experienced the Renaissance or the Reformation. Moreover, the Enlightenment in Russia "began late [and] proceeded fitfully" (James Billington). What most sets Russia apart from the West, however, is her Orthodox faith. As one astute writer has observed, "Orthodoxy is deeply embedded in the Russian soul. It defines a Russian's sense of nation, history and identity" (Nathaniel Davis). That was certainly true of the mature Solzhenitsyn, who returned to the Orthodox faith of his childhood while serving an eight-year sentence in the GULag Archipelago. In the Templeton lecture delivered in London in 1983, he spoke of hearing, as a child, older people attribute the disasters that had befallen revolutionary Russia to the circumstance that "men had forgotten God"—an explanation that he himself had come to accept.

For that reason I have examined the consequences of the atheistic socialism that drove the Russian revolutionary movement and the policies of the Soviet regime. When men forget God, Solzhenitsyn believed, communism or a similar catastrophe is likely to be the fate that awaits them. Thus I have also focused attention on his critique of cultural trends that have emerged in the West at least since the 1960s.

SOLZHENITSYN

REVOLUTION AND WAR

Aleksandr (Sanya) Isaevich Solzhenitsyn was born in Kislovodsk, a resort town in the North Caucasus, on December 11, 1918. His father, Isaaki Solzhenitsyn, survived service in the Great War only to die as a result of a hunting accident at the time of his wife's pregnancy. Thus, while his mother, née Taissia Shcherbak, looked for work in Rostov-on-Don, she placed Aleksandr in the care of his maternal grandparents and aunts Maria and Irina; the latter did her best to instill in the boy the Russian Orthodox faith.

At the time of Aleksandr's birth, Russia was in the throes of a chaotic and savage civil war that pitted the Bolshevik "Reds" against the anti-Bolshevik "Whites," the latter being united by little more than a determination to prevent the communists from consolidating the power they had seized from a weak Provisional Government in October (OS) 1917. The odds were not then in the Bolsheviks' favor. By the summer of 1918, twenty-nine anti-Bolshevik governments were functioning in the lands that had once comprised the Russian Empire.

In addition to these self-proclaimed governments, the Bolsheviks faced a formidable Czech Legion. Originally made up of Russian-born Czechs and Slovaks, the Legion had received permission from the Provisional Government to open its ranks to Czech and Slovak POWs. By the end of 1917, it numbered sixty thousand men and constituted a tough fighting force hostile to the Central Powers, especially Austria-Hungary; the Allies therefore recognized it and placed it under the French High Command. Thanks to negotiations with Thomas Masaryk, who was working for "Czechoslovak" independence, the Bolsheviks granted the Legion permission to move across Siberia to Vladivostok, whence Allied ships were to transport it around the world to France, where it would join in the struggle against the Germans.

Before long, however, Leon Trotsky, the brilliant and ruthless organizer of the Red Army who had not been party to the original negotiations, demanded that all noncommunist Russian officers attached to the Legion be removed and that the Czechs retain only enough arms to defend themselves. Increasingly suspicious, the Czechs hid their weapons and used them when, after a violent clash with some Hungarian prisoners, they turned on local Bolshevik authorities investigating the incident. Trotsky then ordered that any armed Czech or Slovak be shot. As a result hostilities between the Legion and the Bolsheviks broke out all along the Trans-Siberian Railroad line.

To make matters still worse for the Bolsheviks, they faced an Allied intervention. When, in March 1918, they signed the Treaty of Brest-Litovsk with Germany in the hope of gaining "breathing space," the Allies worried that war supplies in Archangel and Vladivostok, supplies they had provided, might fall into German hands. Fearing an attack by the Finns (under German command) on Murmansk—site of a new and relatively ice-free port not far from Archangel—a small British and French force went ashore. Because Murmansk was in the hands of Mensheviks and Socialist Revolutionaries (rival socialist groups), the Bolsheviks initially approved the landing, but they soon had reason to reverse their decision. The Allies had adopted British Major-General F. C. Poole's plan to occupy Archangel and launch a major offensive into the interior. Poole's forces did in fact enter Archangel and quickly established an anti-Bolshevik government.

Nor was that all. On July 6, 1918, US President Woodrow Wilson called a White House meeting of his top advisers and set forth a series of propositions and a program of action. Having learned that the Czech Legion had succeeded in taking Vladivostok, he stated that the United States and other governments were obligated to help its forces form a junction with their compatriots farther to the west. He therefore proposed sending seven thousand troops to Vladivostok, where they would join a comparable number of Japanese troops. The combined force would guard the Czechs' line of communication as they moved west. The United States and Japan would announce publicly that their sole purpose was to aid the Czechs in their fight against German and Austrian prisoners. It was, however, the Bolsheviks with whom the Czechs were at war.

Wilson's decision opened the way for an intervention by troops from the United States, Britain, France, Japan, and other countries. To be sure, some sent token forces only, but Japan dispatched seventy-three thousand men. And even if the purpose of the intervention remained ill-defined—to reopen the eastern front? overthrow the communist regime? secure a foothold in the Far East?—the Bolsheviks could not but be alarmed.

At the time of Solzhenitsyn's birth, then, the Bolsheviks' future hung precariously in the balance. And yet, some things were working in their favor. The various White (anticommunist) forces never coordinated their efforts, and no one of them offered a political program likely to attract the Russian peasantry. The Bolsheviks controlled the central core of the country, and Trotsky had, often by brutal means, molded the Red Army into a formidable fighting force. Moreover, they had in Vladimir Ilyich Ulyanov, called Lenin (from the Lena River in Siberia), a leader who possessed an iron will and who did not hesitate to employ terror in the effort to impose it.

Lenin was born on April 10, 1870, in the Volga city of Simbirsk. His ethnic background, which included Russian, Kalmyk, Jewish, German, and Swedish elements, predisposed him to the cosmopolitanism of his later years. Or perhaps it would be more accurate to say that, although Russian by culture, he never identified with Russia. Solzhenitsyn once wrote that "nothing in his [Lenin's] character, his will, his inclinations made him kin to that [in his view] slovenly, slapdash, eternally drunken country."[1] Whether or not he ever professed any Christian belief—he seems to have taken atheism for granted from an early age—his devout parents, Ilya and Maria Ulyanov, had him baptized in the Russian Orthodox Church. Later in life, he told a comrade that "already in the fifth class in high school [i.e., at age sixteen], I broke sharply with all questions of religion: I took off my cross and threw it in the rubbish bin."[2] At the insistence of his mother-in-law to be, however, he wedded Nadezhda Krupskaya in an Orthodox ceremony in 1898.

Lenin was then in Siberian exile—a militant atheist and revolutionary whose brother Alexander had been executed in 1887 for his participation in a plan to assassinate Tsar Alexander III. His hatred of the tsarist government knew no bounds, and he steeped himself in the literature of revolution: Marx and Engels, but even more important, Nikolai Chernyshevsky, son of a priest and author of the bible of the Russian revolutionary movement: *What Is to Be Done?* His reading of Chernyshevsky and other Russian revolutionaries drove Lenin to embrace the more violent and voluntaristic side of Marxism. It was this that distinguished his followers, the so-called Bolsheviks (or Majority Group), from the more orthodox and deterministic Mensheviks (or Minority Group) within the Russian Social Democratic Party.

Like so many of his revolutionary comrades, Lenin lived in exile for long years. After being detained by the police in St. Petersburg during the summer of 1900, he thought it prudent to leave the country for Western Europe. There, except for a few months at the time of the abortive 1905 revolution, he remained until 1917. His was an endless round of conspiratorial meetings and intraparty controversies, the tone and burden of which Solzhenitsyn was to capture so vividly in *Lenin in Zurich*. Shortly after the outbreak of the Great War, Lenin retreated to neutral Switzerland, a place of refuge for many who were seeking to avoid combat.

Lenin was not the only well-known person residing in wartime Zurich. Tom Stoppard was intrigued by the fact that James Joyce and the Dadaist Tristan Tzara were also living there, and in *Travesties* he turned the coincidence to theatrical account with his customary intelligence and wit. In his acknowledgments Stoppard pointed out that nearly every word Lenin speaks in the play came from his *Collected Writings* or from Krupskaya's *Memories of Lenin*. Certainly the character of Lenin's words concerning Tolstoy ring true: "On the one hand [we have Tolstoy's] merciless criticism of capitalist exploitation, on the other hand the crackpot preaching of submission and of one of the most odious things on earth, namely religion."³

Lenin did not refer merely to the so-called Tolstoyan religion, which accepted the teachings of Jesus but not his divinity. He had uppermost in mind the Russian Orthodox Church that had excommunicated the great writer. For the Church and the historic faith it proclaimed, he knew nothing but hatred; "every religious idea," he once wrote to the writer Maxim Gorky, "every idea of god, even every flirtation with the idea of god is unutterable vileness."⁴ Lenin dreamed of the day when he could answer Voltaire's call: *écraser l'infâme*—but with a vengeance. That day arrived sooner than he expected. In February 1917 the government of Tsar Nicholas II collapsed in the streets of Petrograd, a casualty of, above all else, the war. Two organized powers seemed poised to assume power: the Duma (or parliament) and the Soviet (or council) of Workers' and Soldiers' Deputies.

The Duma leaders were primarily liberals of Western European stamp, while the leaders of the Soviet were socialists, primarily Mensheviks and Socialist Revolutionaries. The Soviet leaders were reluctant to form a provisional government, in part because of the chaos with which they would be confronted, in part because the Mensheviks regarded the uprising as the bourgeois, not the proletarian, revolution. In the end, therefore, it was Duma members who formed a

Provisional Government, ultimately headed by Alexander Kerensky, a member of the Duma (representing the Labor Group—Trudoviks—of the Socialist Revolutionary Party) and the Soviet and, like Lenin, a native of Simbirsk.

Kerensky and the government he led faced near anarchy and uncompromising opposition from the political right and left, especially the Bolsheviks, whose chances of seizing power depended upon Lenin's ruthless leadership. But how was he to reach Russia from Zurich? Fortunately for him, he had won the allegiance of Israel Lazarevich Gelfand, called Parvus, one of the most complex figures in the history of the revolutionary movement. Parvus was many things: a well-educated revolutionary, successful businessman, journalist, and schemer who had established valuable contacts with German intelligence and the German High Command.

Kerensky made a great many mistakes over the months (February to October) of the Provisional Government's existence, but only one of them really mattered: he kept Russia in the war. That alone spelled doom for him and his government, for the Russians had lost the will to fight on. Lenin knew this and recognized that it presented an opportunity to seize power from an unstable and unpopular government. He knew too that he and the Germans had an interest in common: the undermining of the Russian war effort. It was as a result of that interest that the Germans, in one of the greatest blunders of the twentieth century, allowed the Bolshevik leader to return to Russia by train through Germany. Upon his arrival at Petrograd's Finland Station, Lenin announced a program of "Peace, Land, and Bread" and refused any support, even temporary, for the Provisional Government: "All Power," he said, "to the Soviets!"

Lenin, Trotsky, and the Bolsheviks had little difficulty making a second revolution—in reality a coup d'état—in late October 1917; there were fewer defenders of the Kerensky government then than of the tsar's government in February. What had been an obscure group of conspirators was now the government of Russia—or at least it claimed to be. Three years of civil war lay ahead. From the first, however, the despotic nature of the Bolshevik regime was on full display. One of Lenin's first acts was to create the Extraordinary Commission for the Struggle against Counterrevolution and Sabotage—the feared Cheka, or political police. As his biographer, Dmitri Volkogonov, has written: "The true father of the Bolshevik concentration camps, the executions, the mass terror and the 'organs' which stood above the state, was Lenin."[5]

There was no larger target for Lenin and the Bolsheviks than the Russian Orthodox Church. Both as an institution and as the propagator of the faith that lay at the foundation of the Russia that was to be destroyed, the Church was *the* enemy. On February 26, 1918, the new regime decreed the separation of church and state and nationalized all church property, including the Alexander Nevsky Monastery (Lavra), in the Tikhvin Cemetery, where the bones of Dostoevsky, Tchaikovsky, Borodin, and many other cultural luminaries lay buried. Of this action one contemporary wrote: "They shut the Monastery; no services, and pilgrims were not allowed in. Red Guards stood guard. By every portal, people were wailing and crying."[6]

And that was merely the beginning. Later that year the Bolsheviks transformed churches into schools, workers' clubs, cattle yards, car repair shops, and warehouses. They encouraged grassroots attacks on Christian holidays that included mock (atheistic and anti-Christian) "celebrations." They destroyed relics and, in one year, opened the places of repose of sixty-five saints. They seemed to derive particular pleasure from the execution of priests and hierarchs—often in the most sadistic manner. Metropolitan Vladimir of Kiev was mutilated, castrated, and shot, and his corpse left naked for the public to desecrate. Metropolitan Veniamin of St. Petersburg, in line to succeed the patriarch, was doused with cold water in the freezing cold.[7] According to the Cheka's own official data, it put 827 priests to death in the final months of 1918. All of this was "so intolerable for any Russian that many unbelievers began to go to church, distancing themselves psychologically from the persecutors."[8]

Nor, of course, were Christian resisters (or "counterrevolutionaries") spared, and there were many of them. Between 1917 and 1920, in the Ural region alone there were 118 antiregime risings in which clergy took part.[9] That was during the civil war, and thus the Bolsheviks had to wait until 1922 to launch an all-out assault on the Church.

As a result of the civil war, the disastrous economic experiment called "War Communism" and, above all, the "requisitioning" of the peasantry's food and seed stores, famine gripped the land. In June 1921, the government warned, with good reason, that some twenty-five million people faced starvation. When members of the intelligentsia formed a committee to do something, Lenin was unmoved. After all, during the famine of 1891, he had opposed any relief efforts; the famine, he believed, would destroy faith not only in the tsar, but in God.[10]

On July 21, 1921, the Bolshevik government reluctantly legalized the intelligentsia's committee as the "All-Russian Committee for Aid to the Starving." The committee obtained the assistance of the Russian Orthodox Church and international organizations such as the Red Cross, the Quakers, and the American

Relief Association (ARA), headed by Herbert Hoover. That was quite enough, as far as Lenin was concerned; on August 27 he ordered that the committee be dissolved and its members arrested or exiled. "Tomorrow," he said, "we will release a brief governmental communiqué saying that the committee has been dissolved because it refused to work. Instruct all newspapers to begin insulting these people, and heap opprobrium upon them."[11] In place of the committee, the government set up a Central Commission for Help for the Hungry that was as corrupt as it was inefficient; some five million people starved to death in 1921–1922.

This did not trouble Lenin in the least. On the contrary, it presented him with the opportunity for which he had been waiting; he could force the church to contribute to famine relief by handing over its valuables. One of Solzhenitsyn's earliest memories—he must have been three or four—was of being in the church of St. Pantaleimon with his mother when cavalrymen commanded by Semyon Budyonny burst in to confiscate everything of value. The church was willing to donate general property, but it refused to surrender holy vessels; in the textile center of Shuia (March 12–16, 1922), some 150 miles northeast of Moscow, believers resorted to violent resistance, ultimately in vain.

In Lenin's absence the Politburo had voted to delay further confiscations, but the Bolshevik chieftain had other ideas. In a secret letter to Politburo members dated March 19, 1922, Lenin ordered that a resolution be passed at a party congress according to which "the confiscation of valuables, in particular of the richest abbeys, monasteries, and churches, should be conducted with merciless determination, unconditionally stopping at nothing, and in the briefest possible time. The greater the number of representatives of the reactionary clergy and reactionary bourgeoisie we succeed in executing for this reason, the better. We must teach these people a lesson right now, so that they will not dare even to think of any resistance for several decades."[12] He made no mention of aid to the starving, and we now know that most of the confiscated wealth of the church was sent to communist parties abroad in the hope of fomenting world revolution.

The recently chosen (by lot) Patriarch Tikhon, a kind and humble man, affirmed the church's willingness to help those in need but could not but denounce as a sacrilege the seizure of eucharistic objects. In May 1922, therefore, the regime placed him under house arrest in Moscow's Donskoy Monastery, where he was subjected to repeated interrogations and threats. At the same time the "Renovationists" (members of the so-called "Living Church"), led by the heretical priest Aleksandr Vvedensky, deposed him. In their view, the Bolsheviks were establishing the kingdom of God on earth. Marxism, according to Vvedensky, is "the Gospel printed in the atheistic language."[13]

Not every Russian agreed. Lenin knew that there were philosophers, writers, and academics, many of them Christians, who held the living church in contempt. The most prominent among them was Nikolai Berdyaev, born to an aristocratic family in Kiev in 1874. While a student at the University of Kiev, Berdyaev embraced Marxism, though he never warmed to materialism. Before long he felt himself drawn increasingly to questions of a religious nature and to the Orthodox Church, even though he thought it in need of fundamental reform, especially with respect to its conservative politics. Then, too, his Christianity was, according to Oxford lecturer Nicolas Zernov, who knew him, "more prophetic than traditional."[14]

In 1909, in the aftermath of the 1905 revolution, Berdyaev and six likeminded thinkers published *Vekhi* ("Landmarks" or "Signposts"), a devastating critique of the revolutionary intelligentsia. "The atheistic philosophy that had always so attracted the revolutionary intelligentsia," Berdyaev wrote in his contribution, "held nothing as sacred, whereas the intelligentsia gave that same philosophy a sacred character and prized its own materialism and its own atheism in a fanatical, almost Catholic manner."[15] Another contributor, Simeon Frank (a Jewish convert to Orthodoxy), wrote that "by his outlook and way of life the *intelligent* is, above all else, a monk."[16] He and his colleagues called for a spiritual/religious (that is, an inner) transformation as the necessary foundation for any political and social renewal.

Vekhi quickly went through five editions and achieved a *succès de scandale*. The left-wing press described it as an unheard-of betrayal of a sacred heritage and denounced the contributors as enemies of enlightenment and progress. The historian and agnostic Pavel Milyukov called upon readers of the book to come to their senses and "return to the ranks of the intelligentsia."[17] Lenin took time to pen a scathing attack on the volume and its authors.[18]

Berdyaev knew then that Lenin had always looked upon him with disfavor, yet he seems not to have taken the Bolshevik coup very seriously, at least at first. But by 1918, when he opened a religious-philosophical academy in Moscow, he recognized that Russia was staring into the abyss. Inspired by Dostoevsky, on whom he offered an academy seminar, he concluded that, at its deepest level, socialism was more than a socioeconomic ideology—it was a secular religion fully compatible with atheism.

Berdyaev could not publish any of his work after 1918 and was aware that the Bolsheviks looked upon him with an increasingly jaundiced eye, but he had a friend among the regime's leaders—Anatoly Lunacharsky, the commissar of enlightenment (that is, of culture), whom he knew from his time at the university. (Lunacharsky had, in the years before World War I, been a leading "God-Builder," that is the proponent of a secular pseudo-religion.) Moreover, Lenin was preoccupied with the civil war.

By 1922, however, the Bolshevik leader was ready to move against Berdyaev (and other intellectuals whom he despised). Cheka director Feliks Dzerzhinsky himself interrogated the philosopher, but as Solzhenitsyn wrote with admiration, Berdyaev "did not beg or plead. He set forth firmly those religious and moral principles which had led him to refuse to accept the political authority established in Russia."[19] To put him on trial appeared pointless. On the night of August 16–17, 1922, therefore, the GPU (successor to the Cheka) arrested forty-six persons, twenty-one of whom were quickly released after promising to go into exile at their own expense; Berdyaev was among the latter.

On September 28, 1922, Berdyaev and others sailed into exile aboard the specially chartered German ship, the *Oberbürgermeister Haken* (nicknamed the "Philosophy Steamer"). As Lesley Chamberlain has observed, "The 1922 expellees were the first dissidents from Soviet totalitarianism, whose fates would be connected with later individual victims of Soviet banishment like the writer Alexander Solzhenitsyn and the poet Joseph Brodsky."[20] Although Berdyaev and Solzhenitsyn had very different experiences in Soviet Russia and were very different men, they shared a hostility to communist rule and to a soulless West.

Like Dostoevsky, both men were leading critics of Russia's revolutionary tradition. In a piece entitled "Spirits of the Russian Revolution" that he published in 1918, Berdyaev wrote this: "In Russia there took form a special cult of revolutionary sanctity. This cult has its saints, its sacred tradition, its dogmas. And for a long time every doubting of this sacred tradition, every criticism of these dogmas, every non-reverential attitude towards these saints led to an excommunication."[21]

At the beginning of the revolutionary tradition to which Berdyaev referred stood Vissarion Belinsky who, though one of the so-called Westernizers, was not, like Aleksandr Herzen and Mikhail Bakunin, of the nobility; his father was a rural physician. Largely an autodidact, Belinsky established himself through the force of his personality (he was called "furious Vissarion" after Ariosto's *Orlando Furioso*) as an influential literary critic during the repressive reign of Nicholas I (1825–1855). Initially, he convinced himself that Hegel's word that "the real is the rational" meant that he had to accept Russian reality, even as he continued to loath it. Soon, however, he was calling himself a socialist and making of literary criticism a thinly disguised form of radical social criticism, at the center of which was atheism. "It is an important fact," Berdyaev wrote, "that in Belinsky Russian revolutionary socialism was combined emotionally with atheism."[22]

It was not only Belinsky's atheism, but his blasphemy that Dostoevsky could not abide. The great writer never forgot a conversation he had with the critic in 1845. "That man reviled Christ to me in the foulest language, but meanwhile he himself was never capable of setting all the movers and shakers of the whole world side-by-side with Christ by way of comparison. He was not able to notice how much petty vanity, spite, intolerance, irritability, vileness, and most important vanity there was in him and in them."[23]

It was Belinsky's atheism that formed the background to his famous "Letter to N. V. Gogol." He had recognized and appreciated Gogol's genius—until the author of *Dead Souls* published *Selected Passages from Correspondence with Friends* in 1847. Although Gogol seems to have been religious by nature, it was as a result of meetings with Elder Macarius of Optina Monastery that he converted, or deepened his commitment, to the Orthodox faith. "I went," he said, "to the Elder one man, and came out another."[24] He wrote the *Selected Passages* in an effort to clarify his beliefs for his admirers, many of whom took him to be a liberal rather than the conservative he was. Far from being a defense of Russian reality, however, the book called for moral renewal, based upon Christ's injunction to love one another, in all areas of Russian life. It did not call for social or political transformation.

For Belinsky, that was unforgivable. In his "Letter," passed from hand to hand, he deplored Gogol's views, denounced the clergy, described the Russian people as atheistic by nature, and claimed that Voltaire was a truer Christian than any priest. This view became standard; it was embraced by that secular order known as the "intelligentsia" and inspired the next, even more radical, generation of revolutionaries, the leading member of which was Lenin's hero, Nikolai Chernyshevsky.

Chernyshevsky was born in 1828 in Saratov on the Volga. His father was an Orthodox priest who was well read and who, unlike many parish priests, had evinced no interest in revolutionary ideas. Young Nikolai entered Saratov Seminary in 1842 and graduated four years later. Russia's seminaries, Dostoevsky once observed, "produce the most vicious atheists, not to mention quite simply blasphemers. Nobody knows how to blaspheme so thoroughly and skillfully as a seminarian."[25]

If seminary did not destroy whatever belief Chernyshevsky may have retained, further education did. His parents sent him to St. Petersburg University, where he read Ludwig Feuerbach's *Essence of Christianity* and other anti-Christian works. By the time he completed his program of study he had become a convinced atheist, materialist, and socialist. After a time as a teacher at the Saratov *gymnasium*, he joined the editorial staff of the radical journal *The Contemporary* and became a regular contributor.

Because of his outspoken and radical views, the police arrested Chernyshevsky in the summer of 1862. While awaiting trial in the Peter-Paul Fortress, he asked for and received permission to write a novel; in four months—December 1862– April 1863—he wrote: *What Is to Be Done?*

Chernyshevsky had to resort to Aesopian language in order to fool the censors, which, initially, he succeeded in doing. His excruciatingly dull and didactic story revolves around "new people" who show Russians how they should live and how they *would* live after the revolution. The heroine, Vera Pavlovna, is an emancipated woman who leaves her husband, Lopukhov—with whom she had been living as a sister rather than a wife—to marry his best friend, Kirsanov. This she does only after much inner turmoil, Lopukhov's assurance that, given her personality and life circumstances, she was following the only rational course, and his apparent suicide. "Apparent" because Lopukhov, being nothing if not rational, knows that Vera will never feel free to marry Kirsanov while he lives—so he fakes his own death.

But Vera is not only a partner in a new, rational marriage, she is the organizer of a dressmaking workshop and cooperative. She and the young women she hires are equal owners of the workshop and divide the profits evenly. Inspired by Louis Blanc and Robert Owen, though Chernyshevsky could not admit this, Vera's workshop is a model for the utopian economic and social orders of the future; the girls live together in one large apartment and share everything in common.

Lopukhov and Kirsanov both believe in "rational egoism," the notion that all actions are in fact the necessary result of calculations of personal advantage. We are not to think that there is anything wrong with this; on the contrary, straightforward acknowledgment of this reality will lead to a more honest, less hypocritical, world. Both men are, of course, materialists and atheists who belong to a circle of revolutionary friends—though Chernyshevsky could only hint at this. Among their friends is "an extraordinary man"—Rakhmetov, the model of a revolutionary ascetic.

Rakhmetov practices self-denial. A physical fitness fanatic, he does not drink, does not engage in sex, sticks to a highly restricted diet, and sleeps on a bed of nails. From a wealthy family, he supports poor students. His sole purpose in life is to advance the "cause" that is the revolution; he will allow nothing to sidetrack him, not even—and here Chernyshevsky reveals a profound truth about revolutionaries—love. "I must suppress any love in myself," Rakhmetov says.

As Michael R. Katz and William G. Wagner, who introduce Katz's translation of *What Is to Be Done?*, point out, Rakhmetov's biography parallels that of Orthodox saints, especially the fourth-century St. Alexis, the Man of God.[26] The saint—Dostoevsky's favorite—was also an ascetic. He observed a strict fast, wore a hair shirt, forsook his wife on their marriage day, and gave to the poor what little money he possessed after leaving his wealthy parents. All these things, however, he did for Christ, not the revolution.

Chernyshevsky's creation of a secular saint is consistent with the Russian revolutionary movement as a heretical form of Orthodox Christianity—similar forms with inverted contents. He was, like Belinsky and many other Russian revolutionaries, a religious atheist. This is hardly surprising. As Berdyaev observed, "The soul of the Russian people was moulded by the Orthodox Church—it was shaped in a purely religious mould."[27] Chernyshevsky describes the "new people" in *What Is to Be Done?* as "the salt of the salt of the earth."[28] To his disciples Christ said: "You are the salt of the earth" (St. Matthew 5:13).

In 1864 the government convicted Chernyshevsky of subversion and sentenced him to fourteen years (later reduced to seven) at hard labor, followed by permanent exile. Only in June 1889, four months before his death, was he permitted to return to Saratov. His long years in exile made him a martyr for the cause, and this undoubtedly increased the appeal of *What Is to Be Done?* "Under his influence hundreds of people became revolutionaries," Lenin told a comrade in a Swiss café. "He plowed me up more profoundly than anyone else.... After my brother's execution, knowing that Chernyshevsky's novel was one of his favorite books, I really undertook to read it, and I sat over it not for several days but for several weeks. Only then did I understand its depth.... It's a thing that supplies energy for a whole lifetime."[29] It is not surprising, therefore, that he entitled his most famous and important pamphlet *What Is to Be Done?* (1902).

All the revolutionaries who came after Chernyshevsky were ardent readers of *What Is to Be Done?* They were socialists, materialists, and atheists—and ever more addicted to violence, the logical conclusion of their beliefs. The most notorious among them was Sergei Nechaev, author or coauthor (with Mikhail Bakunin) of the "Catechism of a Revolutionist," from which we learn that "in the very depths of his [the revolutionary's] being, not just in words but in deeds, he has broken every tie with the civil order and the whole educated world, with all laws, conventions, generally accepted conditions and morals of this world. He will be an implacable enemy of this world, and if he continues to live in it, that will only be so as to destroy it the more effectively."[30]

There was more. "All tender and debilitating feelings of family, friendship, love, gratitude and even honour must be stifled in him by a single cold passion for the revolutionary cause. For him there can be only one pleasure, one consolation, one reward and one satisfaction—the success of the revolution. Day and night he must have only one thought, one purpose—merciless destruction. Working tirelessly and cold-bloodedly towards this aim, he must always be prepared to die and to destroy with his own hands anything that stands in the way of its achievement."[31]

This was not simply bravado. Nechaev had a rare ability to attract others to his cause. He convinced them that they were part of a vast European-wide revolutionary organization and, by involving them in the murder of an alleged informer, sought to prevent any loss of nerve. Reading of this murder and Nechaev's eventual arrest and trial inspired Dostoevsky to write one of his greatest novels, *The Devils* (also translated as *The Demons* or *The Possessed*). This is a novel about many things, all of them closely related: the revolutionary movement, the conflict between generations, and the problem of religious faith and its loss.

Dostoevsky took for his epigraph the famous story of the Gadarene demoniacs (St. Luke 8:32–36). "Now a herd of many swine was feeding there on the mountain. So they [the demons] begged Him that He would permit them to enter them. And He permitted them. Then the demons went out of the man and entered the swine, and the herd ran violently down the steep place into the lake and drowned. When those who fed them saw what had happened, they fled and told it in the city and in the country. Then they went out to see what had happened, and came to Jesus, and found the man from whom the demons had departed, sitting at the feet of Jesus, clothed and in his right mind. And they were afraid. They also who had seen it told them by what means he who had been demon-possessed was healed."

In the novel Russia's demons (atheistic/socialistic ideas emanating from Western Europe) enter into young radicals, who proceed to self-destruct. They belong to the generation of the 1860s, the sons and daughters of the generation of the 1840s, that of Belinsky and Herzen. Stepan Verkhovensky is a member of the latter generation and an educated hanger-on; Dostoevsky seems to have modeled him after Herzen and the University of Moscow historian T. N. Granovsky. He is a man of progressive ideas, rather than of revolutionary action, a non-Christian with some vague sympathy for Deism. His appreciation of great literature remains, although he has read few serious books since his youth.

His son, Peter, is modeled on Nechaev. He has nothing but contempt for his father and the older generation, spits upon culture, and possesses no religious belief of any kind. Like Nechaev, he pretends to be the local agent of an international revolutionary movement and involves his cell of five in the murder of an alleged informer. He devotes every waking minute to mayhem and destruction—with no discernible purpose. Nevertheless, he finds it rather easy to gain the support of many who fear that they may be thought insufficiently progressive.

Peter Verkhovensky sums these people up this way: "The teacher who laughs with the children at their God and at their cradle is ours already. The barrister who defends an educated murderer by pleading that, being more mentally developed than his victims, he could not help murdering for money, is already one of us. Schoolboys who kill a peasant for the sake of a thrill are ours. The juries who acquit all criminals without distinction are ours. A public prosecutor, who trembles in courts because he is not sufficiently progressive is ours, ours. Administrators, authors—oh, there are lots and lots of us, and they don't know it themselves."[32]

Although Dostoevsky began the novel as an antirevolutionary pamphlet, it eventually became a far more profound work. At its center stands one of the most demonic figures in modern literature—Nikolai Stavrogin. Stavrogin is an atheist who, as is almost always true of Dostoevsky's characters, lives a life consistent with his beliefs, or unbelief. His rule of life is, he says, "that I neither know nor feel good or evil and that I have not only lost any sense of it, but that there is neither good nor evil (which pleased me), and that it is just a prejudice."[33] In keeping with that "rule," he violates a twelve-year-old girl and shows no emotion when he learns that she has hanged herself.

So shocking was Stavrogin's confession of this act to the retired Bishop Tikhon, based upon St. Tikhon Zadonsky, that Dostoevsky's publisher refused to print it; it was found among his papers years after his death. Thus contemporary readers did not learn of the depth of Stavrogin's depravity. Nevertheless, they did learn of the evil influence he exerted on others. Peter Verkhovensky is all but a slave to him; he sees beauty (of the demonic kind) in him and attempts to enlist him in the revolutionary cause—without success, because Stavrogin is unable to commit himself to anything, even to organized destruction.

Because the confession chapter could not be published, Dostoevsky was left without a positive figure. Of the "devils," however, we know this: they have learned atheism from the West and their self-destruction will free Orthodox Russia for its *universal* mission. In his famous address on Pushkin, delivered in 1880 on the occasion of the dedication of the Pushkin monument in Moscow, Dostoevsky declared that to be a genuine Russian was "to utter the ultimate word of great, universal harmony, of the brotherly accord of all nations abiding by the law of Christ's Gospel."[34]

In his "Catechism of a Revolutionist," Nechaev wrote that "for him [i.e., a revolutionary] moral means everything that facilitates the triumph of the revolution; everything that hinders it is immoral and criminal."[35] That was certainly true for Lenin, who never hesitated to destroy everyone and everything that stood in his path—the Orthodox Church and Christians above all. Having forced Berdyaev and other leading religious philosophers into exile, he placed even greater pressure on Tikhon, still recognized as patriarch by the faithful.

In June 1923 Tikhon gave in to pressure. "Henceforth," he wrote, "I am no enemy of the Soviet regime."[36] He died a broken man in 1925 (glorified by the Russian Orthodox Church in 1989). By then Lenin was dead and the church broken to saddle. Because the Soviet regime would not permit the election of a new patriarch, Metropolitan Peter served as *locum tenens* and chose Metropolitan Sergei as his deputy. Within months, however, the police arrested Peter, and Sergei assumed leadership of the Church. In an effort to protect it, he issued a *Declaration* on July 29, 1927, in which he professed the Church's complete loyalty to the Soviet state.

By then the struggle to succeed Lenin waged by Trotsky and Joseph Stalin had been won by the latter, a former seminarian. Born Joseph Djugashvili to a

cobbler and his wife in Gori, Georgia, on December 6 (OS), 1878, Stalin matric-
ulated at the local church school in 1888; it was not long before he began to
entertain doubts concerning the existence of God. Prompted by his mother—
but not his father—and hoping to rise above his humble station in life, Stalin
enrolled in the Tiflis Orthodox Seminary in August 1894. From the first he
despised what by all accounts was a deplorable institution. "I became an atheist
in the first year," he later recalled.[37]

He was not alone. "No secular school," a fellow seminarist recalled, echoing
Dostoevsky, "produced as many atheists as the Tiflis Seminary." An avid reader,
Stalin obtained and read a library of forbidden books, including works by Victor
Hugo, Émile Zola, and many Russian writers. Like Lenin, he was much taken
with *What Is to Be Done?* In May 1899 he either left the monastery on his own
volition or was expelled. He then began his life as revolutionary, bank robber, and
exile. In Siberia in 1915, he attended a meeting with other Bolsheviks; each was
asked to name his greatest pleasure in life. This was Stalin's response: "My greatest
pleasure is to choose one's victim, prepare one's plans minutely, slake an implacable vengeance, and then go to bed. There's nothing sweeter in the world."[38]

In full command of the Soviet Union by 1929, the "man of steel" launched
the so-called Second Revolution, the forced collectivization of agriculture. This
war on the Russian peasantry claimed millions of lives. At the same time, Stalin
intensified the war on the Church. The regime made mass arrests of clergy,
closed churches, and further restricted permissible religious activity. After a
brief easing of pressure between 1932 and 1936, Stalin decided to destroy the
Orthodox Church as an institution. He failed, however, in his attempt to eradicate belief among the laity; believers went underground in houses and other
secret churches.

When that proved impossible, believers prayed the "Jesus Prayer," silently:
"Lord Jesus Christ, Son of God, have mercy on me, a sinner." The prayer is said
in obedience to St. Paul's injunction (in I Thessalonians 5:17) to "pray without ceasing." In the nineteenth-century Russian Orthodox book *The Way of a
Pilgrim*, the pilgrim encounters a *starets* (holy elder), who teaches him the Jesus
prayer, or prayer of the heart. The constant repetition of the prayer is not an
incantation or mantra; rather it puts the pilgrim in direct contact with God.
The prayer is rooted in the tradition of Eastern Christian spirituality, though
its central role in J. D. Salinger's *Franny and Zooey* has helped to make it more
widely known in the West.

From Lenin, Stalin inherited the system of concentration camps that Solzhenitsyn was to call the GULag Archipelago. On August 9, 1918, Lenin sent a telegram to the executive committee of the province of Penza, instructing it to intern "kulaks, priests, White Guards, and other doubtful elements in a concentration camp."[39] In order to bring some system to the growing number of camps, Dzerzhinsky issued decrees on April 15 and May 17, 1919. There was to be at least one camp in each province, with space for a minimum of three hundred people. At the end of the year there were twenty-one camps; at the end of 1920, there were 107.[40]

In 1921, in an effort to find more remote areas, officials looked to Kholmogory and Pertominsk, near Archangel. There they established Northern Special Purpose Camps, in former monasteries. This was perfect; expel the monks and turn the monasteries into prison camps. And yet the new camps proved unsuitable for large concentrations of prisoners. In 1923, therefore, the authorities turned their gaze to the Solovetsky Islands (nicknamed Solovki), an archipelago in the White Sea. There would be far more space, and escape would be all but impossible.

The large main island, Solovetsky, was home to a monastery. As Solzhenitsyn pointed out, the authorities loved "to set up their concentration camps in former monasteries: they were enclosed by strong walls, had good solid buildings, and they were empty. (After all, monks are not human beings and could be tossed out at will.)"[41] Moreover, there was something satisfyingly symbolic about the expropriation—sacred places became secular, state power replaced church authority. For survivors and others, Solovetsky has always been regarded as the first camp of the GULag.

The story of Solovki may be said to begin in 1429, when an aging monk named Savatii and a younger monk named German set out for Solovetsky Island to live as hermits. When, six years later, Savatii reposed, German searched for and found a new brother, Zosima, with whom he planned to build a monastery, rather than a hermitage. In the end, the two established both, a monastery and several hermitages.[42] The community continued to grow, and in 1558 the monks laid the foundation for the Cathedral of the Transfiguration.

Toward the end of the sixteenth century, Russia found herself at endless war with Sweden. When the Swedes learned of the death of Ivan IV ("the Terrible"), who had sent exiles to Solovetsky Island, they began to push their way into the White Sea region, and Solovki had to mount a defense. The new tsar, Fyodor, ordered the monks to build a great fortress, which they did. It served not only as a means of defense but as a prison for traitors, heretics, and rebels. To help defend the main island, soldiers took up residence.

Not long after Peter the Great became tsar in 1682 (technically he was co-tsar until 1696), it occurred to him that Solovki would be an ideal place to send prisoners, including political prisoners. He sent a few dozen, but that was only the beginning. Nicholas I sent greater numbers of prisoners, some of whom were "Decembrists" who had attempted to seize power in Russia on the death of Nicholas's brother, Alexander I, in 1825. The Bolsheviks took control of Solovki as early as 1920 and rounded up monks living on the lesser islands of the archipelago. The following year they closed the monastery and sent all monks, except for the sick and elderly, to the mainland.

On June 1, 1923, the GPU sent the first 150 prisoners to Solovki. With them went an administration for the "Solovetsky Special Purpose Camp" (SLON, which happens to mean "elephant" in Russian). The administration divided the prisoners into three groups: those who had been directly involved in non-Bolshevik politics; counterrevolutionaries (CRs), including members of the clergy; and common criminals. The second group was by far the largest. By the end of 1923, there were "only" three thousand prisoners; and yet they had to be kept in check. How? Solzhenitsyn answered the question. "Only *by terror*! Only with Sekirnaya Hill [a place of punishment]! With poles! With mosquitoes! By being dragged through stumps! By daytime executions![43]

Dmitry Likhachev, the eminent literary scholar and Orthodox believer, was arrested on February 8, 1928, and sent to Solovetsky in early November of the same year. He remained imprisoned on the island for three years, during which he witnessed the terror of which Solzhenitsyn wrote. In his memoirs Likhachev described mass executions that were carried out in the late fall of 1929. "The graves had been dug a day before the shootings. The executioners were drunk. One bullet per victim. Many were buried alive, just a thin layer of earth over them. In the morning the earth on the pit was still moving."[44]

These murders followed in the wake of the communist writer Maxim Gorky's three-day "visit" to Solovetsky in June 1929. "He will give them hell. He will show them! He, the father, will defend!" The prisoners, according to Solzhenitsyn, "awaited Gorky almost like a universal amnesty."[45] Likhachev described how the camp guards prepared a "Potemkin village" for Gorky. They decorated roads, sent prisoners into the woods so that the living space would appear greater, and provided patients in the sick-bay with clean dressing-gowns. They made the punishment cell, the *sekirka*, appear warm and comfortable.

While at Solovetsky, Gorky was approached by a fourteen-year-old boy who told him the truth about the island prison. According to Likhachev, the boy was shot.[46] The irate guards then filled the *sekirka* with new guests and began the mass murders. As for Gorky—he left a hymn of praise for the camp in the "visitors' book" and in *In and About the Soviet Union* he described a "typical" camp guard this way: "From frequent smiles the face of this man had become brighter, as if he had washed it. Now it became clear that his face is good-natured and his dark eyes look at people softly and with trust."[47] The prisoners lived well and were on their way to being reformed. "In some of the rooms," Gorky wrote, he saw "four or six beds, each decorated with personal items ... [and] on the windowsills there are flowers."[48]

None of them lived well, of course, and a great many of them perished, including Father Pavel Florensky, whom Solzhenitsyn called "one of the most remarkable men devoured by the Archipelago of all time."[49] The priest was a renaissance man—theologian, philosopher, art historian, mathematician, philologist, and electrical engineer. In his youth he had established ties with members of the "Silver Age" intelligentsia, including Dmitry Merezhkovsky and wife Zinaida Gippius, but he came in time to be devoted to Russian Orthodoxy and to its vital center at Trinity St. Sergius Monastery. As an ordained priest (1911), he defended that holy place after the revolution. That made him a marked man even as he served as a professor at the Electrical Engineering Institute (where he delivered lectures in his priestly robes).

Accused of "publishing materials against the Soviet system," Fr. Pavel was arrested in 1933 and sent to Solovki the following year. On arrival, he wrote to his wife and children: "My first impressions were very depressing, partly, most probably, from travel-weariness, the rough sea passage, not knowing what would happen next and general disorientation."[50] At the end of October 1937, the Soviets evacuated more than a thousand men to the mainland—Fr. Pavel was among them. The political police charged him with counter-revolutionary Trotskyite propaganda and condemned him to death. On December 8, he was shot in the back of the head and buried in a mass grave in Toksovo, thirty kilometers from Leningrad.[51]

By the mid-twenties, the Bolsheviks had come around to the view that the camp prisoners should be thought of less as candidates for reeducation and more as productive laborers. The country had need of coal, gas, oil, and wood. Why not send prisoners to Siberia and the far north, where these resources were available in abundance? This new insight also brought a certain rationality to the arrests; arrest those with special and needed skills. Under the direction of the OGPU, successor to the GPU, the entire camp system was reorganized and named the Main Administration of Corrective Labor Camps and Labor Settlements—eventually shortened to the Main Camp Administration—*Glavnoe Upravlenie Lagerei* in Russian. Hence the acronym GULag.

Not only did the country need coal, gas, oil, and wood, it needed gold to make purchases abroad, and there was gold to be had in the Kolyma region in the far northeastern corner of Siberia. "I almost left Kolyma out of this book," Solzhenitsyn wrote in *The GULag Archipelago*. "Kolyma was a whole separate continent of the Archipelago, and it deserves its own separate histories."[52] That is just what Robert Conquest provided. Kolyma, the poet/historian wrote in *Kolyma: The Arctic Death Camps*, was to Soviet Russia what Auschwitz was to Nazi Germany, the archetypical place of mass murder.

Late in 1931 the NKVD (the People's Commissariat for Internal Affairs) established Dalstroy, the Far Northern Construction Trust, to oversee road construction to, and mining operations in, Kolyma. At its head the police placed the Latvian communist Eduard Berzin, whose task it was to use prison laborers to extract as much gold as possible. To that end, he treated them in a relatively humane fashion, even if brutal weather conditions took a toll from the first—winter temperatures regularly reached fifty degrees below zero Fahrenheit. By 1937, however, Stalin had decided that Berzin was "coddling" prisoners; he ordered his arrest and execution. From then on, Conquest wrote, the "purpose of Kolyma, which had originally been the production of gold, with death as an unplanned by-product, [became] the production, with at least equal priority, of gold and death."[53]

To gain some sense of what prisoners in Kolyma endured, one has only to turn to the *Kolyma Tales* of Varlam Shalamov. The son of an Orthodox priest, Shalamov fell in with Trotskyites and was arrested in 1929, the year Stalin expelled Trotsky from the Soviet Union. Released after performing over two years of forced labor in the Urals, Shalamov worked as a journalist in Moscow. Arrested again in 1937, he was sent to Kolyma, where he survived (barely) for almost seventeen years. The devastating "tales" that he wrote on the basis of his experiences are, rather than historical fiction, fictionalized history, a genre that Solzhenitsyn himself was to perfect.

Camp prisoners, Shalamov reported, were divided primarily into two groups: common criminals and "politicals" convicted of violating one or another subarticles of Article 58 of the Russian Soviet Federative Socialist Republic penal code; very broadly interpreted, the article covered "counter-revolutionary activity." Common criminals, Shalamov wrote, "did not trouble the government."[54] Quite the contrary. They were "friends of the people," encouraged to commit violent acts against the politicals. "The criminal world, the habitual criminals whose tastes and habits are reflected in the total life-pattern of Kolyma," Shalamov observed, "are mainly responsible for [the] corruption of the human soul."[55]

The politicals, on the other hand, were "enemies of the people" and were treated accordingly by the criminals and the authorities. They were fed little, beaten, and worked to death. Shalamov described mass burials this way: "The bulldozer scraped up the frozen bodies, thousands of bodies of thousands of skeleton-like corpses. Nothing had decayed: the twisted fingers, the pus-filled toes which were reduced to mere stumps after frostbite, the dry skin scratched bloody and eyes burning with a hungry gleam."[56]

How many perished in the Kolyma camps? Based upon a careful study, the details of which he provided, Conquest estimated the total to be at least three million. And "they were, virtually without exception, entirely innocent of the charges brought against them."[57]

One of the common apologies, or explanations, for Soviet forced labor camps and mass murders is that they were simply a continuation of Russian, and tsarist, tradition. This argument will not withstand scrutiny. Conquest concluded that, in the last half century of tsarist rule, there were about 14,000 executions, most of which came after the 1905 revolution during which revolutionaries carried out about four thousand assassinations. Moreover, the detentions and executions under the tsars "were all of people who had committed some offence."[58] "It was," Solzhenitsyn wrote, "in this nearly unanimous consciousness of our innocence that the main distinction rose between us and the hard-labor prisoners of Dostoevsky."[59]

Another way, in fact, to look at tsarist and Soviet Russia is to compare the tsarist *katorga*—forced labor or penal servitude—with the GULag. Dostoevsky served four years in a convict prison at Omsk, Siberia, and later wrote about his experiences in *The House of the Dead*. For his part, Shalamov was unmoved; "there was no Kolyma," he wrote, "in the House of the Dead."[60] Solzhenitsyn agreed: "As for Dostoevsky's hard labor in Omsk, it is clear that in general they simply loafed about."[61] Not that Omsk was a picnic. Never to be alone, even for a single minute, was, for a man like Dostoevsky, a kind of torture. Nevertheless, he and his fellow prisoners were well fed—many of them fasted during Great Lent!—and could even sneak some vodka. They did little work in winter and were able to bring in a priest for the Christmas and Pascha (Easter) Divine Liturgies.

What of Solzhenitsyn during the time so many were suffering in the GULag? As we have seen, his Aunt Irina (even more than his mother) initiated him into the Orthodox faith. According to biographer Michael Scammell, she "taught him the true beauty and meaning of the rituals of the Russian Orthodox church, emphasizing its ancient traditions and continuity. She showed him its importance to Russian history, demonstrating how the history of the church was inextricably intertwined with the history of the nation."[62] Outside of the home, however, he encountered a very different creed—atheistic communism. Indoctrination in that creed was not limited to the classroom; it was also the business of the Young Pioneers and the Komsomol (Communist Union of Youth). The result? "I was brought up in a Christian spirit but youth in the Soviet period took me away from religion entirely."[63] He had become a communist.

And a dedicated one at that. Upon the completion of his *gymnasium* studies, Solzhenitsyn enrolled at Rostov State University, where he majored in physics and mathematics. Because he had a talent for those subjects, he found time to pursue his true interests—literature and dialectical materialism—on his own. In 1939, while still working on his degree, he began correspondence courses at Moscow's Institute of History, Philosophy and Literature (MIFLI), an institution similar in kind to Paris's École normale supérieure. By then he had met Natalya Reshetovskaya, a beautiful chemistry student whom he married by simple state

registration in April 1940; he took a copy of *Das Kapital* on his honeymoon to
Tarusa, a resort some seventy miles south of Moscow. Years later he recalled
that he had tried many times to "fathom the wisdom" of that book—without
success.[64]

In the autumn Solzhenitsyn began his final year at the university, the proud
holder of a Stalin scholarship. He took a first-class degree in mathematics and
physics in the spring of 1941 and in June traveled to Moscow to sit for sec-
ond-year examinations at the MIFLI; he arrived on June 22, a day that changed
his and his country's life forever.

On that day Hitler launched "Operation Barbarossa," war on the Soviet Union.
Despite repeated warnings from the West and his own intelligence network, Stalin refused to take precautionary measures for fear of "provoking" the Führer.
Even when German troops crossed the frontier, his orders were not to return
their fire, for fear of provoking a greater attack.[65] When reports reached him of
a massive invasion he was so stunned that for a time he was all but paralyzed.
By June 28 the Germans had advanced some three hundred miles into Soviet
territory and taken Minsk, the capital of Belorussia; the fall of that city opened
the road to Moscow.

Solzhenitsyn rushed to enlist and was told that he could do so only in Rostov,
where he had lived with his mother since 1924. When, after several days, he was
able to reach his home, he was again disappointed. Because of a slight abdominal defect, he was not permitted to sign up. As a result, he and Natalya took
up teaching positions in Morozovsk, located between Rostov and Stalingrad.
Meanwhile, the war was going from bad to worse for the Russians. In July the
Germans took Smolensk while continuing to advance in the south toward Kiev
and the north toward Leningrad. In September they captured the former and
laid siege to the latter.

Recognizing that he could not rally Russians in defense of communism,
Stalin began to place the struggle in the tradition of historic defenses against
the Teutonic Knights, the Tatars, the Poles, and, of course, Napoleon. This was
a decision of critical importance, particularly when, in November 1941, as the
ground hardened, the Germans launched "Operation Typhoon," the battle for
Moscow. By then the Russians knew that they needed every able-bodied man;
Solzhenitsyn was finally called to arms.

When old, Solzhenitsyn described his years in the army as one of the "most important and defining moments" in his life.[66] It was, however, to be some time before he made it to the front. After several months as a private, he attended officer candidate school and in October 1942 emerged as a commissioned officer who experienced "the happiness of forgetting some of the spiritual subtleties inculcated since childhood."[67] It would be some time before he began to remember them again.

Stalin summoned General Georgi Zhukov to defend Moscow. Born into a peasant family, Zhukov was a veteran of World War I, who joined the Bolshevik Party after the October Revolution. In the early 1920s he presided over the brutal suppression of the Tambov (peasant) rebellion against Soviet power. "It was a full-scale war," Solzhenitsyn wrote in a story/history written in 1994–1995, "and you had to give it all you had, and more. It wasn't like that German War. It was here in Tambov that Yorka [Zhukov] turned savage; it was here that he became a hardened, cruel warrior."[68] Like Stalin, Zhukov never counted the cost in casualties, his own or those of the enemy.

At Khalkhin Gol, the decisive battle in the 1938–1939 (undeclared) border war with Japan, Zhukov established a still wider reputation for his indifference to victory's cost in blood. "Without waiting for artillery and infantry," Solzhenitsyn wrote, "he threw a whole tank division directly at them. Two-thirds of them never made it back, but he gave the Japanese a roasting!"[69] He did not roast the Germans at Leningrad, but he did prevent them from taking the city, and thus Stalin placed the Soviet forces before Moscow under his command. Supply problems, the Russian winter, and the unexpected Soviet offensive of December 5 foiled the Germans' effort to take the capital. Whether or not this was *the* turning point in the war remains an open question, but it was certainly *a* turning point—and a boost to Zhukov's growing reputation.

The war, however, was far from over. Dizzy with success, Stalin ordered an ill-advised and ill-fated offensive on all fronts. Moreover, he persisted in the mistaken belief that the Wehrmacht would strike at Moscow again. Instead, Hitler had decided to head south to the oil fields of the Caucasus and to Stalingrad, where an unimaginable battle awaited his forces. Toward that city drove General Friedrich Paulus and the German Sixth Army. Belatedly aware that he lacked the competence to direct the war, Stalin ordered Zhukov to Stalingrad and promoted him to Deputy Supreme Commander. Much, then, would depend upon Zhukov and Chief of Staff Aleksandr Vasilevsky, the talented son of a village priest.

The Germans launched their attack in August with a Luftwaffe bombing campaign that reduced much of Stalingrad to rubble. As they entered what was left of the city, they were confronted with the nightmare of urban warfare—street fighting, or what they came to call *Rattenkrieg* (war of rats). Vasily Grossman, later the author of the outstanding novel, *Life and Fate,* was in Stalingrad as a correspondent for the Red Army newspaper *Red Star.* He was, historian Antony Beevor has written, "fascinated by the way soldiers watched, learned and improvised new methods to kill the enemy. He was especially interested by the snipers" and got to know Stalingrad's most famous: Vasily Zaitsev.[70]

Neither the Germans nor the Russians asked for or gave any quarter. In the end the combined number of casualties approached two million. Although for a time the Germans controlled 90 percent of the ruined city, the Russians' determined resistance and the extreme winter weather exacted a terrible toll. And on November 19, with the Germans near the end of their tether, the Russians launched Operation Uranus against the Romanian and Italian forces protecting Paulus's Army's flanks. The operation was a success, and the Germans found themselves cut off and surrounded.

They fought on, but the end was near. "Military standards," historian Richard Overy has written, "gave way to a crude instinct for survival. One veteran recalled that in the icy atmosphere the German soldiers were overcome by feelings 'of the bitterest disillusionment, hidden terror and mounting despair.' Food rations were cut to a minimum: two ounces of bread and half an ounce of sugar a day. Occasionally there was horsemeat. The lucky ones caught cats or rats. Rumours of cannibalism persist."[71] On January 31 Paulus surrendered. With victory, Grossman observed, came a new national consciousness. "The history of Russia was no longer the history of the sufferings and humiliations undergone by the workers and peasantry; it was the history of Russian national glory."[72]

As war raged, Solzhenitsyn grew increasingly impatient. He wanted, out of a sense of self-respect and a desire for experience (to be used for future writing), to see combat. This was not an uncommon desire. In his war journal of January 31, 1944, the American soldier (and philosophy PhD) J. Glenn Gray wrote this:

"What is ahead may be grim and dreadful but I shall be spiritually more at rest in the heart of the carnage than somewhere in the rear. Since I have lent myself to the war, I want to pay the price and know it at its worst."[73] The battalion Solzhenitsyn commanded was an important one, trained to plot the position of enemy guns by analyzing their sound waves. "Without any sound reconnaissance," he wrote years later, "the artillery can rarely identify a target. They can only do it in darkness by direct observation of a muzzle flash, and only if the enemy gun position is exposed."[74]

Finally, in April 1943 he and his men received orders to move from the far north to a point east of Orel. They quickly found themselves involved in what the Germans called Operation Citadel, aimed at the Soviet salient (a huge bulge into the German front) around the city of Kursk. Zhukov and Vasilevsky managed to persuade the impatient Stalin to adopt a defensive strategy and made massive preparations. Russian troops and civilians dug some three thousand miles of trenches, set anti-tank traps made from stakes, and laid more than four hundred thousand mines. The armed forces then moved over one million men, three thousand tanks, three thousand planes, and nineteen thousand guns into place. The corresponding German figures were nine hundred thousand, twenty-seven hundred, two thousand, and ten thousand. The greatest tank battle in history began on July 5.[75] It ended in a stalemate, and hence a Russian victory.

The Germans were stunned by what happened next—a Russian offensive that led to the capture of Orel on August 5. Solzhenitsyn's unit formed part of the central front commanded by General Konstantin Rokossovsky, and he himself earned the Order of the Patriotic War, second class. In June 1944 he was promoted to captain, and he and his men found themselves in the thick of battle in Belorussia. On June 29 the Red Army liberated the city of Bobruysk; there Solzhenitsyn experienced a moment in what one may call his spiritual reawakening. He heard a man cry out to him for help—a Russian wearing German britches; Solzhenitsyn described him as a "Vlasov man," in reference to General Andrei Vlasov, whose Second Shock Army had been left by Stalin to be destroyed behind German lines. After being captured, Vlasov chose to fight for Germany in the hope of liberating Russia from totalitarian rule.

The "Vlasov man" cried out as he was being lashed on his naked back. Solzhenitsyn was disgusted but lacked the courage to intervene. "*I said nothing and I did nothing. I passed him by as if I could not hear him.*" That picture, he wrote in *The GULag Archipelago*, "will remain etched in my mind forever."[76] So did the hanging of an accused Russian traitor that he witnessed in the Belorussian village of Besed. He described that event in chapter five of *The Trail* (*The Road, The Way*), a poetic autobiography of over seven thousand lines that he composed in his head and memorized while in captivity between 1947 and 1952.

Solzhenitsyn explained in *The GULag Archipelago* how, using a rosary-like set of "beads" (pieces of cork), he carried out this remarkable feat of memory. "No longer burdened with frivolous and superfluous knowledge, a prisoner's memory is astonishingly capacious, and can expand indefinitely. We have too little faith in memory!"[77] This new appreciation for the possibilities and importance of memory never left Solzhenitsyn. It inspired him to devote his life to restoring his country's memory—historical and spiritual. He understood that the great ambition of totalitarianism is "the total possession and control of human memory"[78] and recalled what George Orwell wrote in *Nineteen Eighty-Four*: "who controls the past controls the future: who controls the present controls the past."

By the end of 1944, Soviet forces had crossed into Poland, where they met little resistance from the weakened German army. In January 1945 they entered East Prussia, having been told by Stalin that everything was permitted. They took him at his word; in the ensuing months, they looted at will and raped some two million German women. "Imagine a man," Stalin said to the Yugoslav communist Milovan Djilas, "who has fought from Stalingrad to Belgrade—over thousands of kilometers of his own devastated land, across the dead bodies of his comrades and dearest ones. How can such a man react normally? And what is so awful about his having fun with a woman after such horrors?"[79]

In East Prussia Solzhenitsyn's spiritual reawakening continued as he gained greater insight into the power of sin, over others and himself. We know this from *Prussian Nights*, chapter nine of *The Trail*. The poem recounts looting, by him and others. But there were greater evils. "All of us knew very well," he wrote in *The GULag Archipelago*, "that if the girls were German they could be raped and then shot. This was almost a combat distinction."[80] He enters a burned-out house in which a woman and her dead daughter have been gang raped; the woman begs to be shot. Later he chooses from among several women one to satisfy his lust. "And after, unnaturally close/To the pale blue of her eyes,/I said to her—too late—'How base!'" She begs him not to shoot her. "Have no fear. . . . For—Oh!—already/Another's soul is on my soul . . ."[81]

Did Solzhenitsyn commit this act? The protagonist of *The Trail* is "Sergei Nerzhin," who could well be a composite and slightly fictionalized figure. But the other events described are clearly autobiographical, and the final lines of "Prussian Nights" were left out of the version published in Russian in 1974 and in English translation in 1977.

Where are you, pure light of childhood?
The flicker of the icon-lamp?
The silvery gleam of the Christmas tree?
Is it not a murderer and a rapist
Who is now reaching for a pen?

———————————

I step forth to repent publicly
In the numbing cold of popular contempt.[82]

CHAPTER TWO

IN THE GULAG

S olzhenitsyn's war ended abruptly on February 9, 1945. Summoned to the office of Brigadier-General Zakhar Travkin, he was placed under arrest for critical remarks he had made about Stalin in an incautious correspondence with Nikolai Vitkevich, an old school friend. In their letters, the two men had charged the *Vozhd* (leader) with betraying the cause of the Revolution, calling him *pakhan*, a head of a criminal organization.[1] For the next two years, the "Organs" (as the political police liked to call themselves) detained Solzhenitsyn in various Soviet prisons, beginning with Moscow's notorious Lubyanka, where, to his surprise, he found a good library. He was there when, in May, the war in Europe came to an end. In June, however, he was moved to Butyrka prison, also in Moscow. There, in the following month, the "Special Commission of the NKVD" sentenced him to eight years in the GULag.

At the time the sentence was considered light, but Solzhenitsyn could not but be dismayed at the prospect of so many years in captivity. Nevertheless, there were reasons why, years later, he looked back upon his prison life with some feeling of gratitude. For one thing, it furthered his—slow—spiritual awakening. In Butyrka he met Boris Gammerov, a prisoner who had served in an antitank unit during the war. They began a conversation, in the midst of which Solzhenitsyn seized the opportunity to sneer at a prayer, said to have been offered by the late President Roosevelt: "Well, that's hypocrisy, of course." Much to his surprise, Gammerov challenged his cynicism: "Why do you not admit the possibility that a political leader might sincerely believe in God?" Stunned, Solzhenitsyn asked the young man if he believed in God. "Of course," Gammerov replied.[2]

In early August 1945 the Organs again transferred Solzhenitsyn, this time to the Krasnaya Presnya transit prison elsewhere in Moscow. The prison served as the embarkation point for the vast GULag Archipelago. There he encountered, for the first time, the common criminals whom the political prisoners referred to as "friends of the regime" because of the relatively favorable treatment they received.[3] The criminals organized themselves into a gang, the better to rob and intimidate politicals such as Solzhenitsyn, who quickly discovered that he lacked the courage to confront or challenge them. He knew then that he was entering a state of nature in which the only law was that of the jungle.

But that was not the only lesson he learned in the transit prison. A "special-assignment" prisoner taught him that he must, at all costs, avoid "general-assignment" work, the main detail in any given camp. "Eighty percent of the prisoners work at it [general-assignment]," he was told, "and they all die off. . . . The only ones who *survive* in camps are those who try at any price not to be put on general-assignment work."[4]

Solzhenitsyn did not long remain in Krasnaya Presnya. Within a month his keepers transferred him to New Jerusalem, a former monastery transformed into a corrective labor camp west of Moscow. Here he got his first taste of forced labor, working in the clay pits of a brick factory. By his side was Gammerov, who had also been moved—but only for a time. The young man soon succumbed to tuberculosis. "His spiritual image was lofty," Solzhenitsyn recalled, "and [the verses he wrote] seemed to me very powerful at the time."[5]

Solzhenitsyn was more fortunate. Because New Jerusalem was scheduled to become a camp for German POWs, the authorities moved all the surviving *zeks* (slang for prisoners); after only three weeks, they sent Solzhenitsyn on to Kaluga Gate, on the south side of Moscow. There he succeeded in talking himself into a position as a "works manager," which meant that he was housed in a special trusty's room. On the lookout for any advantage, he joined the camp's theatrical group, which made it possible for him to mix with women, with one of whom, Anya Breslavskaya, he conducted an affair. His time at Kaluga was not, however, a romantic idyll; he often worked ten hours a day laying parquet floors. Worse, he agreed, under pressure, to act as an informer—though he apparently never did so.

On July 18, 1946, the authorities ordered Solzhenitsyn to prepare for another move—back to Butyrka, where, among other prisoners, he met Yevgeny Divnich, an Orthodox priest. "He did not confine himself to theology," Solzhenitsyn remembered, "but condemned Marxism, declaring that no one in Europe had taken it seriously for a long while." Solzhenitsyn defended the dogma; "after all I was a Marxist." But he argued with less conviction than in the past.[6]

Before leaving Kaluga Gate Solzhenitsyn had filled out a form in which he brazenly declared himself to be a "nuclear physicist." He knew of the Soviets' interest in the atomic bomb and gambled that he could bluff his way into a better situation. The gamble paid off. In September 1946 the authorities sent him to a *sharashka* (a prison scientific research institute) in Rybinsk on the upper Volga. Five months later, his keepers sent him to Zagorsk, outside of Moscow, where he worked as a librarian. Finally, on July 9, 1947, he was sent to the *sharashka* at Marfino, next to Ostankino Park on the outskirts of Moscow. There he was to remain for almost three years.

Much of what we know of his life at the Marfino *sharashka* derives from *In the First Circle*, the novel he wrote between 1955 and 1958 (with later revisions). The title refers to the first circle of hell in Dante's *Inferno*—a place of less torment than in the lower circles, but still hell. The years at the *sharashka* are crucial for an understanding of Solzhenitsyn's spiritual awakening and of his growing sense of mission; it was during that time that he resolved never to forget the evil done by the communist regime, much less those who suffered as a result of it. Gleb Nerzhin, an alter ego in the novel, feels that "he had a duty to discharge, a mission to carry out, for all of them. He knew that it was not in his own obstinate nature to be deflected, to cool off, to forget."[7]

The novel made some of Solzhenitsyn's *sharashka* coworkers famous. Not long after he arrived at Marfino, he met Dmitri Panin, an engineer whom he called Dmitri Sologdin in the novel. In his memoirs, Panin recalled that first encounter. "I shall never forget the first thing he said to me: 'As I was coming down the stairs, what should I see in the darkness of the lobby but an image of the Savior Not-Made-by Hand[s].'"[8] The image to which Solzhenitsyn referred, of which Panin apparently bore a resemblance, is one of the earliest of the Holy Icons. According to Orthodox tradition, Abgar, ruler in the Syrian city of Edessa during the time of Christ, suffered from leprosy. A believer, he sent his court painter, Ananias, to paint an image of the Savior, but because of the crowds he failed in his mission. Having noticed him, however, Christ wiped his face with a wet towel, and on it was impressed His divine image. He then gave the towel to Ananias to take back to Edessa; Abgar was healed and later baptized.

As Solzhenitsyn was soon to learn, his reference to Panin's physical resemblance to the Savior Not-Made-by Hands was apposite; his new friend was a devout Christian who despised the Bolshevik regime. "We must," Sologdin tells Nerzhin, "have the courage to see the evil in the world and to root it out.

Wait a while—you, too, will come to God. Your refusal to believe in anything is no position for a thinking man; it's just spiritual poverty." Nerzhin remains unconverted, but he does speak vaguely of "some sort of Higher Reason in the universe." He had, as a result of his prison experiences, lost his faith in Marxism, but that only increased his fear of being deceived again; better to maintain a healthy skepticism. "Skepticism," he argues, "is a way of silencing fanaticism; skepticism is a way of liberating dogmatic minds."[9]

But it is not only dogmas of which Nerzhin is skeptical. He has come to think that truth about ultimate matters cannot be found simply, or even primarily, through reason, but only through experience. That is why, though he knew the unhappiness of years of detention, he "was secretly happy in his unhappiness. He drank from it as from a fresh spring. In this place he had gained an understanding of people and of events not to be had elsewhere." Prison "was not just a curse—it was also a blessing."[10]

This was especially true for Solzhenitsyn, an aspiring writer who hoped one day to reveal the truth about the Russian Revolution, to expose the lies foisted upon the Russian people. He recognized that Stalin counted upon his ability to make people forget what really happened to them and to their country. "Whole nations behaved like Queen Anne in Shakespeare's *Richard III*: Their wrath was short-lived, their will infirm, their memory weak, and they would always be glad to give themselves to the victor." Ironically, there was no better place to discover the truth concerning the revolution and the communist "experiment" than "through the bars it had set in place."[11]

Not every one of Nerzhin/Solzhenitsyn's friends agreed, of course. Lev Rubin (real name Lev Kopelev) remained indignant about his unjust imprisonment but continued to cling to the communist faith to which he had committed himself as a young man. In the early 1930s Kopelev was among the activists sent to the villages to coerce the peasants into joining the collective farms. "I was convinced of my ideological superiority to the peasants," he wrote years later, "and was ashamed of feeling pity while we robbed them." Why that was so he tried to explain to himself and others. "We were raised as the fantastical adepts of a new creed, the only true *religion* of scientific socialism. The party became our church militant, bequeathing to all mankind eternal salvation, eternal peace and bliss of earthly paradise."[12]

After serving as a propaganda officer in World War II, Kopelev was arrested for protesting the mistreatment of German civilians by Soviet soldiers; he served ten years in the GULag. Even during that time, however, he "stubbornly believed, wanted to believe, that the cruel baseness and dull heartlessness of our organs of state security, procurators, judges and prison and camp officials, as well as the shameless lies of our press, official propaganda, and official literature—all were merely unnatural, irregular perversions."[13] "If something is still wrong [in the country]," he told Dmitri Panin, "then it is just a matter of putting it right."[14] In Solzhenitsyn's novel, Kopelev/Rubin defends his faith more fiercely than Christians—Sologdin excepted—defend theirs. According to Panin, the debates he and Kopelev engaged in were far more intense than those between Rubin and Sologdin in the novel.

Perhaps that is because Solzhenitsyn read Kopelev's soul so perfectly. After one debate with Sologdin, Rubin reflects upon the undeniable fact that, under Soviet rule, the foundations of morality had been sapped. That, he knows in his heart of hearts, was because the regime had driven Christianity, a sure foundation for morality, from public life. He could not, as a Jew, will a Christian revival, but he does prepare a "Proposal for the Establishment of Civic Places of Worship," complete with "temple attendants" (*not*, he emphasizes, priests), to be submitted to the Central Committee of the Party. An atheist, he fears that Dostoevsky was right: if God is dead, everything is permitted.

Solzhenitsyn usually remained on the sidelines during the Panin-Kopelev debates, but he listened intently and discerned irony in the fact that such an open exchange of views could never occur on the outside! Another benefit of detention. On occasion he seized the opportunity to debate Kopelev. In the novel Nerzhin is particularly incensed by Rubin's insistence that all enlightened minds had embraced socialism. "All the greatest thinkers in the West! Sartre, for instance! They all support socialism! They're all against capitalism! That's almost a platitude by now! You're the only one who can't see it! *Pithecanthropus erectus!*" Nerzhin replies that talk of "socialism" and "capitalism" is meaningless. He prefers to speak of "a family of one's own," "the inviolability of the person," or most important, "moral self-limitation."[15]

Although Nerzhin, Sologdin, and Rubin manage to find time to debate, they have work to do, including devising a "scrambler" phone that Stalin could use without fear of someone listening in. A more important task is to identify the traitor who, on the phone, had attempted to warn the West that an American spy was planning to hand over atomic secrets to a Soviet agent. Solzhenitsyn did not invent this, but he did invent the character who made the call—Innokenty

Volodin, another of his alter egos. Like his creator (before his arrest), Volodin is a Marxist and an unthinking servant of the regime.

In time, however, this dutiful diplomat begins to be dissatisfied with his marriage, his work, and his privileged but empty existence. That dissatisfaction soon attaches itself to Soviet life in general, and knowing of the planned espionage, he decides, on the spur of the moment, to alert the American embassy. This reckless act releases a new person, one in search of a more authentic life. Never having felt much affection for his deceased mother, Volodin finds himself rummaging through the letters and diaries she left behind; they trigger an epiphany. In them he reads words (written in capital letters) such as Truth, Goodness, Beauty, Good, and Evil—words not to be found in the Soviet man's vocabulary.

In addition to the letters and diaries, Volodin stumbles upon stacks of magazines of which he had never heard. In them he encounters the names of European writers and publishing houses—also new to him. Before his eyes, the world of prerevolutionary Russia opens up. As a consequence, he begins to ask himself questions. Why had the February revolution, a genuine uprising that brought down the tsar's government, been tossed down the memory hole? Why was the October (Bolshevik) revolution, called a coup even by Soviet books in the 1920s, hailed as the greatest revolutionary event in human history? The truth suddenly dawns on him: "There was no elemental, nationwide flare-up in October; all that happened was that the conspirators assembled at a given signal."[16]

Volodin was at last in a position to appreciate the life and wisdom of his Uncle Avenir, whom he visits in Tver. The old man ekes out a poverty-level living by working with his hands. Willing to speak openly of his total rejection of the Soviet regime and all its works, Uncle Avenir explains that he could not, in good conscience, perform any kind of official work. "Everything I do here I do with a clear conscience. When I empty the slops, it's with a clear conscience. I scrape the floor with a clear conscience. If I rake out the ashes and light the stove, there's nothing bad in that. But if you've got a position to hold down, you can't live like that. You have to truckle . . . and you have to be dishonest."[17]

That the old man speaks for Solzhenitsyn is beyond any doubt; it is a view adopted in the novel by both of his alter egos: Volodin and Nerzhin. "His [Nerzhin's] aim now was to become ordinary, to shed the affectations—the exaggerated politeness, the preciosity—of the intellectuals. In the years of unrelieved disaster, in the worst moments of his shattered life, Nerzhin decided that the only valuable, the only important people were those who worked with their hands, planing timber, shaping metal, tilling the soil, smelting iron. He tried now to learn from simple laboring people the wisdom of their infinitely skillful hands and their philosophy of life."[18]

By the time the Organs arrest and subject Volodin to the humiliating physical "examinations" and interrogations to which Solzhenitsyn himself was subjected, he is a new man, at peace with himself at last. Nerzhin too is at peace, even when the Organs send him to one of the "special camps" in which political prisoners performed hard labor. And so were Solzhenitsyn and Panin when, on May 19, 1950, they were ordered to prepare themselves for transfer to a special camp. As difficult as it may be to believe, Solzhenitsyn had begun to find his relatively easy life in the *sharashka* distasteful. For one thing, he had recognized his calling as a writer and wanted to experience the lower circles of hell, the worst of the camps. For another, he wanted to try his soul, to ignore the advice once given him by the special-assignment prisoner: "At all costs steer clear of general duties."[19]

By the time he began the three-month trek to his new "home," Solzhenitsyn was no longer married. Natalya could not advance, or even maintain, her career at the scientific laboratory where she worked if she were married to a political prisoner. But there was more to it than that. Over the years, the two had drifted apart, not least because, as he knew from their previous lives together, she could not begin to understand, much less accept, his growing interest in religion. This spiritual distance was now accompanied by a geographical distance; sometime during the third week of August 1950, Solzhenitsyn arrived at the special camp at Ekibastuz on the barren steppes of Kazakhstan in Soviet Central Asia.

The story of Solzhenitsyn's almost three years at Ekibastuz was one of conversion or, as he put it, of "ascent." From the moment of his arrival, he resolved not to devote his thoughts and efforts to becoming a trusty with special privileges but to acquire a skill and perform hard labor. It sickened him to think that as a member of the intellectual classes, he never learned to work with his hands. The meaning of his life, of *life*, could not be found by mere cerebration. He set out to make of himself a smelter and a bricklayer, to go "where the calm and simple people go."[20] That day, he later wrote, "was the beginning of the most important years in my life, the years which put the finishing touches to my character."[21]

It should come as no surprise, therefore, that the protagonist in *One Day in the Life of Ivan Denisovich*, written in 1959, is a bricklayer in a special camp resembling Ekibastuz. Nor is it a surprise that Ivan Denisovich Shukhov is a peasant with no formal education. He is serving ten years for having escaped from a German POW camp, where, the Organs insisted, he had been recruited to spy. We follow one day in his life, a day filled with cold, hunger, hard work, and little hope; and yet he is at peace with himself and with his fate. What were pitifully small things to readers who never knew, and never would know, life in the GULag were blessings to Shukhov—an extra piece of bread, a little more time out of the cold, a cigarette. As for the hard work of bricklaying—"it wasn't all that cold outside. A great day for bricklaying."[22]

A simple man, Shukhov believes in God, but not for theological, much less rational, reasons. "So you believe in God, do you, Shukhov," the captain of his "gang" of workers asks him with a smile. "Of course I do," he replies. "How can anybody not believe in God when it thunders?"[23] Not a sophisticated faith, but as Solzhenitsyn wanted his readers to know, a real one. Shukhov is particularly fond of Alyoshka, a young Baptist who has been sentenced to twenty-five years for his faith. Based upon Anatoly Silin, a Baptist poet whom Solzhenitsyn met in Ekibastuz, Alyoshka is completely at peace with himself. He will do anything to help someone else, without any thought of advantage or reward.

Alyoshka teaches Shukhov that he should never pray for worldly or transient things, other than his daily bread. "What people prize highly is vile in the sight of God! We must pray for spiritual things, asking God to remove the scum of evil from our hearts." That is all well and good, Shukhov tells the boy, but such prayers won't reduce your sentence by as much as a day. Alyoshka's reply comes straight from Solzhenitsyn's heart; it is confessional. "What good is freedom to you? If you're free, your faith will soon be choked by thorns! Be glad you're in prison. Here you have time to think about your soul."[24] (It cannot be accidental that "Alyosha" and "Ivan" are the names of Karamazov brothers who engage in intense spiritual exchanges.)

In the famous section "The Soul and Barbed Wire," in *The GULag Archipelago*, Solzhenitsyn reemphasizes this point. "The meaning of earthly existence lies not, as we have grown used to thinking, in prospering, but . . . in the development of the soul."[25] Paradoxically, he insists that that development is aided, not hindered, by suffering. It was only as he suffered in the camp at Ekibastuz that Solzhenitsyn found genuine friendship and seriously reconsidered his previous life, including the evil he had done.

Varlam Shalamov took a very different view of the camp experience. "All human emotions," he insisted, "love, friendship, envy, love of one's fellows, mercy, thirst for fame, honesty—fell away from us along with the meat of our muscles."[26] Solzhenitsyn did not deny that many *zeks* were corrupted, "but not only because the camps were awful, but because in addition we Soviet people stepped upon the soil of the Archipelago spiritually disarmed." Those who had a religious faith, he insisted, were not corrupted; many of them perished, but their souls remained pure. Would it not be more correct to say then that "no camp can corrupt those who have a stable nucleus, who do not accept that pitiful ideology which holds that 'human beings are created for happiness,' an ideology which is done in by the first blow of the work assigner's cudgel?"[27]

As though the tribulations of camp life were not enough, Solzhenitsyn discovered a swelling on his right groin in December 1951; camp doctors diagnosed him with cancer. He knew that he might be facing death when he underwent surgery on February 12, 1952. At the time, it is important to note, he had not yet come to view the link between suffering and redemption in strictly Christian terms. But as he lay recovering in the camp hospital, he was visited by a Jewish doctor, Boris Nikolayevich Kornfeld (not his surgeon), who spoke at length of *his* conversion to Christianity. That same night someone murdered the physician in his sleep.

As he continued his recovery in the hospital, Solzhenitsyn formed his latest thoughts into verses. In them he reflected upon his "arrogant brain" and his loss of faith; he concluded with these lines:

> And now with measuring cup returned to me,
> Scooping up the living water,
> God of the Universe! I believe again!
> Though I renounced You, You were with me![28]

Although, as Solzhenitsyn knew, the Orthodox Church views salvation as a process, not a single moment of decision, this was certainly a critical juncture in his life, a time of spiritual renewal and previously unknown wisdom. "Gradually," he wrote much later, "it was disclosed to me that the line separating good and evil passes not through states, nor between classes, nor between political parties either—but right through every human heart."[29] It was, then, a reborn man whom the authorities released to perpetual exile on February 13, 1953—the same month that his divorce from Natalya became official. After another interminable journey Solzhenitsyn arrived in his new "home" of Kok-Terek on the edge of a Kazakhstan desert. The date was March 3, 1953; two days later, Stalin died.

Solzhenitsyn did not learn of the tyrant's death until the following day, March 6. That was "the moment for which every *zek* in GULag (except the orthodox Communists) had prayed," he wrote in *The GULag Archipelago*. "He's dead, the dictator is dead! The villain has curled up and died!"[30] The Soviet Union was about to change, not overnight and not beyond recognition, but slowly and significantly.

In the meanwhile, Solzhenitsyn needed work. In the hope of obtaining a teaching position, he contacted the district education department, only to learn that the local high school was fully staffed. Living in a primitive hut on the small amount of money given him by GULag officials, he used his time to write, with a freedom he had never before known. Soon, however, he would have to do his writing in the evening. Knowing of his background in mathematics, the district consumer cooperative employed him—but not for long. In April the regional director of education appointed him teacher of mathematics, physics, and astronomy at Kirov High School in the village of Berlik; he assumed his duties on May 3.

"Shall I describe the happiness it gave me," he wrote later, "to go into the classroom and pick up the chalk? This was really the day of my release, the restoration of my citizenship."[31] His joy, however, was to be short-lived. Before long, he began to experience abdominal pain; a doctor in the hospital in nearby Dzhambul confirmed that the cancer had returned and advised him that he had only weeks to live. One can imagine the depression that descended upon him: "It seemed as though for me life, and literature, was ending right there. I felt cheated."[32] On January 4, 1954, he entered a cancer ward at the Tashkent Medical Institute.

The resident oncologists prescribed massive doses of radiation, along with hormonal treatments. By mid-March Solzhenitsyn was feeling much better; he was discharged but not yet cured. Before returning to Kok-Terek, he entered an Orthodox church and thanked God for his new lease on life. In June he returned to Tashkent for further radiation treatments; they rid him of the cancer. Having come face to face with death, he remained very much alive—and able to turn his experience in Tashkent to literary account. In 1968 he published, in the West, an extraordinary novel: *Cancer Ward*, set in Tashkent in 1955. Stalin has been dead for two years, and so has Lavrenti Beria, the vicious and depraved NKVD chief. Georgi Malenkov, Stalin's putative heir, has just "expressed a wish" to be relieved of his duties. Change is in the air.

The cancer ward of the title, like the TB sanatorium in Thomas Mann's *Magic Mountain*, constitutes a world of its own, one stripped of nonessentials and in which death is an ever-present reality. Patients have neither the time nor the wish for empty talk. Each in his own way seeks to know "what men live by," the title of a chapter that Solzhenitsyn borrowed from a short story by Tolstoy. In Tolstoy's telling, a shoemaker and his wife, after some initial hesitation, show compassion and love for a naked stranger who turns out to be the angel (Archangel) Michael. From the humble couple Michael comes to understand "that men only think that they live by caring only about themselves: in reality they live by love alone. He who dwells in love dwells in God, and God in him, for God is love."[33]

The main character in *Cancer Ward*, Oleg Kostoglotov, is another Solzhenitsyn alter ego. A veteran of the war, prison, and the camps, he has little use for formal education, of which he possesses no more than a smattering. Life and his fellow prisoners have been his teachers. Every evening in Butyrka Prison, for example, "there were lectures given by professors, doctors of philosophy and people who were experts on some subject."[34] He listened attentively to those lectures for one reason only—to try to understand what men live by, or rather what they ought to live by. His is a profoundly moral view of life. He wants to be able to live with a clear conscience; length of days is secondary.

Not surprisingly, therefore, the oncologists and nurses in the cancer ward find him to be a difficult patient, one who insists upon knowing and understanding everything being done to cure him of his cancer. When he learns, after refusing to be put off, that the hormone therapy will render him impotent, he rebels. "To preserve his life," he asks, "should a man pay everything that gives it color, scent and excitement? Can one accept a life of digestion, respiration, muscular and brain activity—and nothing more?"[35] By extension, ought a man to survive in a totalitarian state by lying, fawning, and betraying others? Patient Shulubin did just that, and he tells Kostoglotov how bitterly he regrets it. A university professor, he feared arrest and so confessed his "mistakes." But that was not enough. "We were supposed to give up lecturing? Very well, I gave up lecturing." He became an assistant, then a librarian, then a book burner. Why? Because he wanted to live.[36]

Patient Pavel Nikolayevich Rusanov, a Stalinist apparatchik, denounced innocent people out of ambition rather than fear. Kostoglotov regards him as a "moral monstrosity" and seizes every opportunity to challenge him. When Rusanov opines that there is nothing worse than cancer, Kostoglotov suggests leprosy. "It's worse because they banish you from the world while you are still alive. They tear you from your family and put you behind barbed wire."[37] Not even the rather obtuse Rusanov could miss the point, and it unnerves him because word of the beginnings of de-Stalinization has reached him and he worries that those being released from the camps might include a former "friend" whom he had denounced.

Rusanov is somewhat relieved when his daughter, a poet very much in tune with the regime, assures him that he has nothing to worry about. Solzhenitsyn paints a hilarious portrait of this young woman—and in that way of hack writers. She is annoyed by young Dyomka, a patient who possesses a genuine love of literature, because he can't seem to grasp the Stalinist writers' vision. "You must understand this," she tells him. "Describing something that exists is much easier than describing something that doesn't exist, even though you know it's going to exist. What we see today with the unaided human eye is not necessarily the truth. The truth is what we *must* be, what is going to happen tomorrow. Our wonderful tomorrow is what writers ought to be describing today."[38]

Kostoglotov sees in Dyomka hope for the future. In a note he sends the young man after being discharged from the cancer institute, he tells him to "get better and live up to your ideals. I'm relying on you." For himself, Kostoglotov has only modest hopes, or perhaps not so modest. He hopes to live out a simple life, clear of conscience, as an exile in the village of Ush-Terek. There he has friends, the Kadmins, who have also been in the camps. They take delight in simple things—a loaf of white bread, a book found in a small bookshop, a movie, a sunset. They love their dogs and cats. "Nowadays we don't think much of a man's love for an animal; we laugh at people who are attached to cats. But if we stop loving animals, aren't we bound to stop loving humans too?"[39]

Solzhenitsyn knew the answer to that question, and he wanted his readers to know it as well. That is what makes two pivotal events in the novel so devastating. First, Kostoglotov learns from the Kadmins that someone has shot their dog. Even worse, on his first day out of the cancer ward, he visits the Tashkent zoo and comes up to the empty cage of the Macaque rhesus monkey. A sign informs visitors that the monkey was blinded by an "evil man" who threw tobacco into his eyes. Kostoglotov is struck dumb and wants to scream: "Why? Thrown just like that! Why? It's senseless!"[40] And so was the GULag.

Like Kostoglotov, Solzhenitsyn returned from the cancer ward to his village exile, there to teach and to write. His initial effort was a play entitled *The Love Girl and the Innocent*. It is set in a camp similar to Kaluga Gate; the time is autumn 1945. Once again, Solzhenitsyn created two alter egos, both of whom are officers and war veterans. The play revolves around the romance between the "innocent" Rodion Nemov (one of the alter egos) and the "love girl" Lyuba Nyegnevitskaya (modeled after Anya Breslavskaya, with whom, we recall, Solzhenitsyn had had an affair).

As the play opens, Nemov is a "works manager" with a guilty conscience. When a woman tells him how pleased the other prisoners are that the job is being "held by a man of education, by an intellectual, not some labour-camp lout," he fires back, "I'm no intellectual! I served four years in the army, and now I'm a prisoner." Soon he is asking himself, "What did I want to go and become one of the bosses for? I thought it was like the army—Officer." To his relief, he loses his privileged position and joins the smelters; "I feel freer now I'm an ordinary black-faced working man."[41]

The importance of a clear conscience, a recurrent Solzhenitsyn theme, stands at the center of the play. "Are our lives so important? Are they the most valuable thing we have?" Nemov asks Lyuba. "What else is there?" Nemov replies: "It sounds funny talking about it here in the camp, but maybe ... conscience...." Granya Zybina, another woman who, despite all she has had to endure, shares Nemov's resolve to place conscience above self-interest. "I made my decision," she says, "I'm not going to live like other people do in the camps. There's only one important thing—I won't see myself turned into a bastard."[42]

Solzhenitsyn's other alter ego, Pavel Gai, is also a man of conscience and, like his creator, he has disciplined his memory. When one of the foundrymen, Grishka Chegenyov, tells Gai of a prisoner about to die, they have this exchange. Chegenyov: "Old Igor isn't going to last. He's written a letter home. To say goodbye." Gai: "To his wife?" Chegenyov: "No, his sister. He didn't have time to get himself a wife. They shot his father in '37. His mother died in the camps. They've got us by the throat. What are we going to do?" Gai: "What can we do? Remember—that's all." Later, when Granya, who loves him, tells him that she too fought in the war, Gai says, "They'll give you an amnesty. In a year you'll have forgotten the whole thing [the war and the camps]." Granya: "So will you." Gai: "Oh no, I won't forget."[43] Neither would Solzhenitsyn.

Having secured regular employment, Solzhenitsyn was in a position to purchase a modest little clay house and a short-wave radio on which he could listen to broadcasts from the West. "We were so worn out by decades of lying nonsense," he wrote in *The GULag Archipelago*, "we yearned for any scrap of truth, however tattered—and yet this work was not worth the time I wasted on it: the infantile West had no riches of wisdom or courage to bestow on those of us who were nurtured by the Archipelago."[44] That conviction never left him.

However disappointed he was in the West, Solzhenitsyn remained content with his life in Kok-Terek. He could teach and write, and he had sufficient money for his modest needs and desires. Meanwhile, on the larger Soviet stage, change was continuing. In the struggle to succeed Stalin, Nikita Khrushchev emerged the victor, and on February 25, 1956, he delivered the now famous de-Stalinization speech to the Twentieth Party Congress. A few weeks later, Solzhenitsyn learned that his sentence had been annulled and his exile lifted.

THORN IN THEIR SIDE

Free at last, Solzhenitsyn completed the school year in Kok-Terek and on June 20, 1956, boarded a train for Moscow. There he was met by Dmitri Panin and Lev Kopelev and there, two days after his arrival, he came face to face with Natalya, to whom, he found, his heart still responded, even though she had been living with Vsevolod Somov, a widower and colleague. Not being able to tolerate the thought of living in the capital or any other large city, he hoped to find a teaching position somewhere in the Vladimir region, some 130 miles to the east. The education officer with whom he spoke in Moscow found a post that might fill the bill for him in Torfoprodukt. On arrival, he found the possible living accommodations unappealing, but the nearby village of Miltsevo seemed ideal for the writing he intended to do.

After some searching, Solzhenitsyn rented space in a rundown house owned by a sixty-year-old widow named Matryona Zakharova, who inspired one of his most beautiful short stories—"Matryona's Home" (1959).[1] It is the summer of 1956 in the village of Talnovo, near Torfoprodukt. The widow Matryona takes Ignatich in as a boarder. He had served years in the GULag, is a teacher, and in the evenings a writer. The house is infested with cockroaches, and Matryona cares for a mangy cat and a goat. All six of the children she bore died in infancy.

The woman knows the meaning of suffering, but she never complains, works herself to the bone, and lends a hand to her neighbors without expecting or asking for anything in return (for which friends and family revile her). Unlike so many, she gives no thought to the accumulation of material things; she is, Ignatich begins to understand, a saintly woman. Though not outwardly religious, she has a good heart. She is not aware of this but her face, Ignatich observes, shows that she is "at ease" with her conscience. And so she is to the end. In the story, as in reality, Matryona dies as a result of a tragic accident.

Solzhenitsyn ends the story on a powerful and moving note. "We had [Ignatich says] all lived side by side with her and never understood that she was that righteous one without whom, as the proverb says, no village can stand. Nor any city. Nor our whole land."

While living in Matryona's house, Solzhenitsyn persuaded a willing Natalya to leave Somov and to remarry. This was accomplished on February 2, 1957, and after completing the school year in Torfoprodukt, he joined Natalya, who was teaching chemistry at the Agricultural Institute in Ryazan. In September he assumed a new teaching position at City High School No. 2, while continuing work on *In the First Circle*. He did not alter the pattern of his life, which was one of work and semi-monastic living, and it did not take long for this to drive a wedge between man and wife. Natalya made efforts to respect her husband's need for peace and quiet, but she had become accustomed to an active social life.

In May 1959 Solzhenitsyn hit upon the idea of writing a novel about a day in the life of a GULag prisoner in a camp much like that at Ekibastuz—what was to become *One Day in the Life of Ivan Denisovich*. He wrote it "for the drawer" in forty days.[2] But the restricted but nonetheless real "thaw" under Khrushchev (so named after Ilya Ehrenburg's novel *The Thaw*, 1954) made him wonder— might it not be possible to get *One Day* (then titled *Shch-854*, Shukhov's *zek* number) published? As an underground writer, he missed having readers competent to judge his work. "In 1961," he later recalled, "after the twenty-second Congress of the USSR Communist Party and [Aleksandr] Tvardovsky's [reform-minded] speech at this, I decided to emerge and offer *One Day in the Life of Ivan Denisovich*."[3]

What happened next is well known. Lev Kopelev brought the "lightened" (that is, expurgated) manuscript to Tvardovsky, editor of the literary journal *Novy Mir*, who knew instantly that Russia had a new and major writer. Because of its theme, however, he also knew that permission to publish would be difficult to obtain, especially after Solzhenitsyn refused to make anything but the most minor cuts and changes. He therefore began to gather appraisals of the work from the most authoritative writers of the day. The great poet Anna Akhmatova's judgment must have encouraged Solzhenitsyn. "Every single citizen of the two hundred million inhabitants of the Soviet Union has the duty to read this text and commit it to memory!"[4]

With strong support from Akhmatova and others, Tvardovsky managed to get the manuscript into the hands of Vladimir Lebedev, Khrushchev's adviser on cultural matters; Lebedev passed it on to his boss. Not knowing that he was bringing to prominence a man who would shake the very foundations of the USSR, the dictator approved publication of *One Day*; "it is," he mused, "a life-affirming work. In fact I'll go so far as to say that it expresses the Party spirit."[5]

One Day appeared in *Novy Mir* in November 1962 and was an overnight sensation. In the blinking of an eye, Solzhenitsyn went from being an obscure teacher and former *zek* to a celebrated writer. Particularly gratifying to him were the letters he began to receive from other former camp prisoners. When the Writers' Union admitted him to membership, he was able to free himself from teaching responsibilities and devote full time to writing. Meanwhile, Tvardovsky, feeling as though he had a free hand with respect to Solzhenitsyn's work, published "Matryona's House," and "An Incident at Krechetovka Station" in the January 1963 number of *Novy Mir*.

These stories did not meet with universal praise from Party writers. More important, Khrushchev had begun to have second thoughts about his approval of *One Day*'s publication. In early March 1963 he delivered to selected writers and artists a threatening speech in which he warned against taking de-Stalinization too far. With reference to *One Day*, his remarks were pointed and characteristically crude: "Take my word for it, this is a very dangerous theme. It's the kind of 'stew' that will attract flies like a carcass, enormous fat flies; all sorts of bourgeois scum from abroad will come crawling all over it."[6]

Fortunately, long and bitter experience had taught Solzhenitsyn to remain cautious and secretive, even when he seemed to be on top of the world. He did not, therefore, broadcast the fact that he was working at a fever pitch on four major projects: *The GULag Archipelago*; *R-17* (which was to become *The Red Wheel*); *Cancer Ward*; and a lightened version of *In the First Circle*. Fearing that these unpublished and explosive manuscripts might one day fall into KGB hands, and knowing that they would not be safe in his possession, he looked for hiding places. He thought immediately of Nikolai Ivanovich Kobozev, under whose guidance his wife had pursued graduate studies in chemistry.

Solzhenitsyn described Kobozev as an Orthodox Christian "acutely aware of the Russian spiritual collapse in the twentieth century." The two men quickly established a relationship of mutual trust, and Solzhenitsyn allowed his new friend to read his unpublished work, while mentioning the difficulty he had in safeguarding it. Kobozev responded by offering to arrange for its storage at a secure location, and from 1962 to 1969, he remained the primary guardian of all of Solzhenitsyn's major works.[7]

The primary, but not the only guardian. Solzhenitsyn entrusted a second set of typescripts and microfilm to Veniamin and Susanna Teush in Moscow. While working at the Institute, Natalya came to know the Teushes, who were Jews and mathematicians, and she continued her friendship with them when they moved to the capital. As a result, Solzhenitsyn made their acquaintance and found that they had lost their Stalinist faith. Nevertheless, like so many of Solzhenitsyn's initial admirers, they remained creatures of the left. Veniamin Teush had no sympathy for the White cause in the civil war, thought the collective farms a real advance in agricultural life, and spoke with bitterness of the "historical crimes of the Church." Even so, Solzhenitsyn, desperate for readers, let the couple read the manuscript of what, in 1960, was still *Shch-854*. Their favorable reaction persuaded him, after the publication of *One Day*, to use their home as a backup security site.

One of the reasons that Solzhenitsyn was so security conscious was his awareness of Khrushchev's erratic behavior. While presiding over a thaw in Soviet cultural life, the dictator had, in 1959, launched a new persecution of the Orthodox Church. "We'll take god by the beard," he said in speeches.[8] During the first years following Stalin's death, the regime had shown greater tolerance of religion, but before long Khrushchev, Leonid Ilyichev (chairman of the ideological commission of the Central Committee), and Mikhail Suslov (the Party's chief ideologue) became cognizant of a spiritual revival and a dramatic increase in church attendance. "We cannot," Ilyichev warned, "be complacent.... It is imperative to oppose religion with militant, progressive, scientific-atheistic propaganda."[9]

In his speech to the Twenty-Second Congress of the Communist Party of the Soviet Union, in session from October 17 to October 31, 1961, Khrushchev insisted that "we need a considered and well-balanced system of scientific atheist education which would embrace all strata and groups of the population and prevent the spread of religious views, especially among children and adolescents."[10] The fear that young people were being led away from "science" and atheism was, for good reason, particularly great among Soviet rulers.

They therefore took a series of steps to prevent it. They instructed priests to refuse the Holy Mysteries (Communion) to children, banned religious instruction to minors, and deprived Christian parents of their parental rights. They refused to intervene when Christian children suffered harassment and physical mistreatment at school. They made determined efforts to infuse atheism in classrooms, ordering that specialized courses be developed and special textbooks produced to emphasize the atheistic implications of all subjects at all levels.[11]

Having unchallenged cultural hegemony, the regime enlisted the mass media in its campaign to indoctrinate children—and adults. Books on atheism proliferated, as did propagandistic articles in newspapers and journals. The journal *Science and Religion*, devoted to the eradication of religion, began publication in 1959. Radio, television, and films promoted atheism and portrayed religion as a dangerous superstition.

Nor was the assault limited to the realm of culture. Employing "legal" means, including those whose purpose was to create insolvency, the regime forced the closing of thousands of churches, including all of those that had spontaneously reopened in territories occupied by German troops during World War II. It declared the sale of candles, lighted and set before icons by the faithful, to be an illegal form of trade. "Inspectors" declared church buildings to be "dilapidated" and required that they be restored—at impossible expense. For fear of contagion, the authorities ordered the closing of any church in proximity to a school.[12] "Town planners" invoked the pressing need to close churches, and every effort was made to prevent priests from performing duties other than conducting services in the churches that remained. Monasteries drew particular attention from the atheistic crusaders because of their well-known spiritual importance to the faithful. Their numbers dropped from about ninety in the mid-1950s to seventeen or eighteen a decade later.[13]

Solzhenitsyn was aware of the regime's effort to eradicate Christianity once and for all, but he had all he could do to advance the work to which he knew he had been called. For one thing, he felt increasingly alienated from Natalya—and she from him. For another, he recognized that his time in favor with the regime had come to an end. His fears only increased when, on October 14, 1964, Leonid Brezhnev, KGB head Vladimir Semichastny, and other Party leaders ousted Khrushchev, who among other sins had precipitated the Cuban missile crisis of October 1962. Brezhnev assumed responsibility as Party leader, while Alexei Kosygin became premier.

"It was Khrushchev's fall," Solzhenitsyn wrote in his memoir, *The Oak and the Calf*, "that drove me into action to safeguard my writings."[14] He sent *In the First Circle* to the West—and a good thing he did. On September 11, 1965, the KGB descended upon the Teushes and their friend Ilya Zilberberg (to whom, on their own, they had entrusted some of the archive) and confiscated the manuscript of

First Circle, along with two plays, a long poem, and a number of "miniatures."[15] Solzhenitsyn was so devastated that he contemplated suicide; he never quite forgave the Teushes, who had been something less than cautious.

To make matters even worse, at almost the same time that word reached him of the KGB seizure of his archive, he learned that the agency had arrested the writers Andrei Sinyavsky and Yuli Daniel, both of whom had published work deemed anti-Soviet in the West. The fact that the men had adopted pseudonyms proved that they had violated Section 1 of Article 70 of the criminal code of the Russian Republic, which prohibited "agitation or propaganda carried out with the purpose of subverting or weakening the Soviet regime or in order to commit particularly dangerous crimes against the state, the dissemination for the said purpose of slanderous inventions defamatory to the Soviet political and social system, as well as the dissemination or production or harboring for the said purposes of literature of similar content."[16]

The four-day trial opened in Moscow on February 10, 1966. In the case of Sinyavsky, who had adopted the pseudonym "Abram Tertz," the prosecution identified three works of "slander": the fictional works *The Trial Begins* and *Lyubimov* and the essay *On Socialist Realism*. In the latter, Sinyavsky characterized the Russian nineteenth century as one suffering from godlessness, with a resulting search for faith. "Culture was made by a handful of mournful skeptics who thirsted for God simply because they had no God."[17]

It was that thirst that led many members of the intelligentsia to embrace Marxism as a "new religion." True, Marxism was atheistic, but "a consistent atheism, an extreme and inflexible denial of God, resembles religion more than [a] vague incertitude." The literature of the new religion demanded "positive heroes," not the "superfluous men" of the troubled and conflicted nineteenth century. In fact, Sinyavsky argued, "socialist realism" preferred open adherents of the old religion. "After all, the enemy was like the positive hero—clear, straightforward, and, in his own way, purposeful. Only his significance was negative—to hinder the movement to the Purpose. But the superfluous man was a creature of different psychological dimensions, inaccessible to computation and regimentation. He is neither for the Purpose nor against the Purpose—he is outside the Purpose."[18]

Sinyavsky was describing himself. During his appearance in court, he reiterated that "Purpose" was central to Soviet society and literature, another way of saying that Marxism was a substitute religion, one he did not pretend to believe (in fact, he had received baptism as an adult). He was quick to add, however, that "the West has been unable to put forward anything like it."[19] His own position he described as "idealistic" and his writings as experiments in "fantastic," not "socialist," realism.

Sinyavsky's friend and co-defendant, Yuli Daniel, adopted the pseudonym "Nikolai Arzhak" and wrote in the realist tradition. The prosecution listed four anti-Soviet works from his pen, all of which had been published abroad. The most important of the four was the brilliant and shattering short story "Hands."[20] The protagonist is explaining to a friend that after he had fought for the Reds in the civil war, the Cheka "mobilized" and assigned him to the Special Service Section, "or, to put it in ordinary language, they made me carry out executions." That, he quickly learned, was not the same as fighting at the front where "either you get him or he gets you. But here . . ."

He describes to his friend how he went about his work. He walked behind the victim and tried to convince himself that what he was about to do could not be helped. "It is necessary. If you don't finish him off, he, that reptile, will overturn the entire Soviet Republic. I got used to it. I drank while I was doing it, of course, you can't do it without drinks." After months on the job, he was ordered to "liquidate a bunch of priests." It had "something to do with that Patriarch, Tikhon." This was going to be a particularly difficult day, not because he was afraid or because he had "some kind of weakness for religion. Nothing like it, I'm a hard man, a Party man, I don't believe in any gods, angels or archangels—and yet I began to feel faint."

He shoots two priests and then forces himself to vomit. He takes a third one into the yard, but when he fires, the priest does not fall. In fact, he turns and starts to walk toward his would-be executioner. The latter fires again and again, but the priest shows no sign of falling and yells: "Your hands are covered with blood! Look at your hands!" Horrified, the assassin collapses from nervous shock. Only later does he learn that his co-murderers, as a joke, loaded his Mauser with blanks. There was no miracle then, and the hospital to which he was sent in shock "cured everything, except for one thing: my hands—you can see it yourself—still shake."

At the trial, Daniel spoke repeatedly of the horrors of the Stalinist years and his fear of a new reign of terror. He told the court that "Lenin [unlike Stalin] was opposed to murder, terror and persecution," but he did not believe that. In subsequent testimony he pointed out that "according to Lenin, revolution is coercion, and the state is coercive."[21] He was being disingenuous too when he insisted that "Hands" was not anti-Soviet; it is nothing if not an indictment of

a cold and murderous regime. In his final plea, he did, however, put the prosecution on the defensive by pointing out that a scene, similar to that in "Hands,"
could be found in Mikhail Sholokhov's *And Quiet Flows the Don*.

Sholokhov, an unrepentant hardliner who had won the Nobel Prize in
Literature the year before, was not amused. At the Twenty-Third Congress of
the Communist Party of the Soviet Union, held in Moscow from March 29 to
April 8, 1966—that is, after Sinyavsky and Daniel had been sentenced to hard
labor for seven and five years respectively—he complained because the two men
had gotten off so easily. "I see here delegates from the party organization of
our dear Soviet Army. What would they have done if traitors had appeared in
one of their units?" Or what if the traitors had been caught in "the memorable
twenties" and tried "in accordance with revolutionary justice?" But now, "if you
please, people talk about the sentence being too harsh."[22]

In an open letter to Sholokhov, sent to the Writers' Union (from which she
was later expelled) and to the editors of several publications, the courageous
editor, writer, and poet Lidia Chukovskaya denounced his "shameful speech,"
which "will not be forgotten by history." Nevertheless, she was capable of writing that trying people "on the basis of 'rough justice' was fitting and natural
during the civil war, in the immediate aftermath of the Revolution," but not in
the present day.[23] Members of the liberal intelligentsia like Chukovskaya, who
idolized Aleksandr Herzen, wanted no return to Stalinism, but they had not lost
their faith in socialism.

By the time Chukovskaya wrote her open letter, her daughter Elena, called
Lyusha, had become what amounted to Solzhenitsyn's private secretary. For six
years, beginning in 1965, she "was the point of intersection for every strand,
every contact, for everything that needed asking, answering, or transmitting."
There is no doubt that she was one of the most important of Solzhenitsyn's
"invisible allies," but like her mother, she remained a "progressive" at heart.
"After more than six years of working together," Solzhenitsyn later wrote in
sadness, "it became apparent that we did not think alike."[24] She was, he noted,
particularly hostile to Orthodoxy and Russian patriotism.

On December 15, 1965—that is, shortly before the Sinyavsky-Daniel trial, which
Solzhenitsyn followed on a transistor radio, two priests, Frs. Nikolai Eshliman
and Gleb Yakunin, addressed a protest letter to Nikolai Podgorny (chairman of
the Presidium of the Supreme Soviet), Alexei Kosygin (chairman of the Council

of Ministers), and Roman Rudenko (chief prosecutor of the USSR).[25] Calling
attention to the January 23, 1918, decree "On Separation of Church and State,"
the April 18, 1929, decree "On Religious Associations," and Article 124 of the
Soviet Constitution, the priests protested illegal actions taken by officials of the
Council on the Affairs of the Russian Orthodox Church.

The priests asserted that the council, created to serve as an organ of media-
tion between church and state, had under Khrushchev been transformed into an
organ of control of the Church. They listed among its illegal actions the closing
of churches and monasteries, the registration through baptism and other rites
of the religious affiliation of citizens for the purpose of discrimination against
them, restrictions on religious practice beyond the confines of church buildings,
restrictions on children's participation in the life of the Church, and interference
in parish financial affairs. That council officials knew they were acting in viola-
tion of Soviet law was demonstrated by the fact that their practice was to issue
unofficial verbal orders.

This letter to the civilian authorities was preceded by Frs. Nikolai and Gleb's
scathing letter to Patriarch Alexei I, in which they listed the same council ille-
galities while charging the patriarch and other ecclesiastical authorities with
silence before—and even active connivance with—atheist officials.[26] Instead
of following the holy example of Patriarch Tikhon, contemporary hierarchs,
including Alexei himself, chose the compromising path taken by Sergius
when he was *locum tenens* (1928–1943). It was the patriarch's duty, the priests
declared, to demand a reversal of the state's illegal actions and to convene an
all-Russian general church council. "The suffering church turns to you with
hope. You have been invested with the staff of primatial authority. You have the
power as Patriarch to put an end to this lawlessness with one word! Do this!"[27]

Alexei did no such thing, though there is evidence that he thought his critics
were right. He chastised the priests for disturbing the peace of the church and
attempting to lead her into error. When they continued to defend themselves
and their letter, he forbade them "to fulfill their office as priests until they fully
repent."[28] Most members of the clergy supported the patriarch's decision.

Solzhenitsyn, however, did not. He had read the protest letter with what he
described as "delight." The priests, he wrote in *The Oak and the Calf*, were courageous and honest voices in defense of a church "which of old had lacked and
lacks now both the skill and the will to defend itself. I read, and was envious.
Why had I not done something like this myself, why was I so unenterprising?"
He resolved to "do something similar!"[29]

And so he did in a "Lenten Letter" to Alexei I's successor, Patriarch Pimen I, dated the third week of Great Lent (Veneration of the Cross), 1972.[30] "It will," he wrote, "soon be seven years since the two righteous priests Yakunin and Eshliman wrote their celebrated letter to your predecessor, confirming, by their sacrifice and example, that the pure flame of Christian faith has not been extinguished in our land. . . . And how were they answered? In the most simple and brutal manner: they were punished for the truth—and prohibited from serving in church. And you have not remedied this to this very day."

That being the case, Solzhenitsyn repeated some of the priests' charges—that the "registration" of those who bring their children to be baptized had discriminatory aims, that unconscionable restrictions were placed upon children's participation in the life of the church, that priests could perform their duties only within the confines of the church, and that atheist officials of the Council for Religious Affairs were ruling the Church—"a spectacle unseen in two thousand years."

Solzhenitsyn was even more concerned by the result of the long years of atheist rule: "We are losing the last traces and signs of a Christian people." At Pascha in April 1966, he was staying at the Chukovskys' dacha at Peredelkino, a writers' colony several kilometers southwest of Moscow, where Boris Pasternak had lived. He walked to the Church of the Transfiguration shortly before midnight, when the priest would shout "Christ is Risen!" There, as believers prepared for the traditional procession, he was greeted by a spectacle he never forgot—a milling crowd of girls dressed as for a Saturday night dance and boys full of drink, with cigarettes stuck to their lower lips.

The attitude of the young was one of an almost studied disrespect and contempt for those who had come to celebrate Christ's resurrection. After all, their "right not to believe in God is safeguarded by the constitution." To be sure, "these are not the militant atheists of the thirties, who snatched the consecrated Easter cakes out of people's hands, dancing and caterwauling and pretending to be devils. This generation is just idly inquisitive. The ice-hockey season on television is over, the football [soccer] season has not started yet, and what brings them to church is sheer boredom." They try to entertain themselves by screaming obscenities and instilling fear in the worshipers. "These millions we have bred and reared," he asked himself, "what will become of them? Where have the enlightened efforts and the inspiring visions of great thinkers led us? What good can we expect of our future generations?"[31]

It was that question along with his disappointment with the Church hierarchy's passivity in the face of the atheist state's attacks that attracted Solzhenitsyn to Fr. Aleksandr Men. Born to a Jewish family, Men was baptized as an infant—along with his mother. Something of a renaissance man, he read religious thinkers such as Berdyaev, Bulgakov, and Vladimir Soloviev, but he had also studied for three years at the Irkutsk Agricultural Institute, where for a time he shared an apartment with Gleb Yakunin, who was then an atheist; Men was instrumental in the latter's eventual turn to the Orthodox faith.

Always devout, Men was ordained a priest in 1960 and began a remarkable ministry that lasted until he was murdered, perhaps by the KGB, in 1990. Always a parish priest, Fr. Aleksandr's fame began to spread among those "new believers" who were beginning to turn from the official atheism. Among his spiritual children were Nadezhda Mandelstam, widow of the famous poet, and the popular bard Aleksandr Galich, "along with members of the Union of Soviet Writers, the Soviet Filmmakers' Union, academic institutes, and agencies of propaganda and education." Years later, the Russian medievalist Sergei Averintsev remembered Fr. Aleksandr as "the man sent from God to be a missionary for the wild tribe of the Soviet intelligentsia."[32]

In the late 1960s the priest met Solzhenitsyn, who was charmed. "Fr Aleksandr," Solzhenitsyn wrote in his memoirs, "was the spiritual leader of a faction that, though still small, was seeking its path within the Soviet-dominated Russian Orthodox church. He conducted unofficial seminars and was mentor to a group of young people."[33]

The meeting took place not by chance. Solzhenitsyn was looking for channels by which he could send copies of his work abroad, and Fr. Aleksandr had one. Her name was Anastasia Borisovna (called Asya) Durova. Born in Russia before the Revolution, Asya Durova and her family emigrated to France in 1919. She studied at St. Mary's School in Neuilly, converted to Catholicism, and became a nun. Never, however, did she lose her love for the land of her birth. When in 1964 she was offered a post in the French embassy in Moscow, she accepted without hesitation. Two years later, she met Fr. Aleksandr and agreed to bring him, from abroad, religious books banned by the Soviet regime.

Not long afterwards, Asya managed to send the manuscript of Fr. Aleksandr's book, *The Son of Man*, to a contact in Belgium; it was this contact that interested Solzhenitsyn. "I asked him whether he would help," Solzhenitsyn recalled. "He agreed readily and with great assurance: 'Yes, of course, *my channel* is still working smoothly."[34] Asya had already begun to extend her work. Along with Hélène Zamoïska, she "passed on" works by Sinyavsky and Daniel. Rather than use diplomats, she sent things with casual acquaintances, often without telling them what they were taking out of the country. Solzhenitsyn availed himself of her "services," with important success.

Fr. Aleksandr Men's reputation quite naturally brought him to the attention of the KGB, which placed him under continuous surveillance. This was a distinction that he shared with Solzhenitsyn, who was a far greater thorn in the side of the security officials. In a "Memorandum on Surveillance Materials Concerning the Attitudes of the Writer Aleksandr Solzhenitsyn," dated October 2, 1965, they reported a conversation he had with Veniamin Teush: "This is a government without prospects. They have no conveyor belts connecting them to ideology, or the masses, or the economy, or foreign policy, or to the world communist movement—nothing. The levers to all the conveyor belts have broken down and don't function."[35]

The duel between Solzhenitsyn and the KGB intensified on May 18, 1967, when the Javert-like Yuri Andropov took over as chairman of the Committee for State Security. In discussion after discussion, memorandum after memorandum, Andropov called for Solzhenitsyn to be prosecuted or expelled from the country. Previous methods such as the campaign of slander and the blacklisting by journals and book publishers were not enough. To Solzhenitsyn, of course, they were intolerable, and he refused to remain a silent victim. In a letter to the Fourth Congress of the Union of Soviet Writers, dated May 16, 1967, he lodged a forceful protest.[36]

After reminding Union members of the censorship, slander, and repression of such outstanding writers as Anna Akhmatova, Sergei Yesenin, Boris Pasternak, Osip Mandelstam, and Vasily Grossman, Solzhenitsyn proposed that the congress demand the abolition of all censorship and indicate its resolve to defend writers who were being slandered and persecuted unjustly. He then protested the ongoing campaign of slander being waged against him and his inability to find publishers for *Cancer Ward* and other works. He did not, however, mention the work that he had all but finished and that he knew had no chance of being published—*The GULag Archipelago: An Experiment in Literary Investigation.* (By "literary investigation" Solzhenitsyn meant the connecting of facts by aesthetic means.) George Kennan was to describe this work as "the greatest and most powerful single indictment of a political regime ever to be leveled in modern times."[37]

Solzhenitsyn dedicated *The GULag Archipelago,* most of which he wrote in
Tartu, Estonia, over the winters of 1965–1966 and 1966–1967, "to all those who
did not live to tell it. And may they please forgive me for not having seen it all
nor remembered it all, for not having divined all of it." He had no trouble tracing
the origins of Soviet terror and the vast labor-camp system back to Lenin, and
to Feliks Dzerzhinsky's Cheka as that system's chief administrative organ, but
he confessed that he could not say why, in his third year at university, he had
refused to fill out an application form for the NKVD. After all, it was clear to
him that "the struggle against the internal enemy was a crucial battlefront, and
to share in it was an honorable task."[38]

He had spared himself the fate of becoming a cog in the terror machine, but
for some inexplicable reason. Was he, moreover, a much better man when he
became an army officer? Looking back upon his prideful and sometimes brutal
attitude and behavior while in uniform, he was not so sure. "I credited myself
with unselfish dedication. But meanwhile I had been thoroughly prepared to
be an executioner. And if I had gotten into an NKVD school under [Nikolai]
Yezhov, maybe I would have matured just in time for [Lavrenti] Beria."[39] Had he
not been arrested, his life might well have continued along a characteristically
"Soviet" path.

In the time available to him in his first prison cell, however, he began to
rethink his entire life—though not his commitment to Marxism or reverence
for the Revolution, which he continued to regard as "magnificent and just."[40]
It was the Revolution and the *ideology* that inspired it, he eventually came to
recognize, that had transformed all of Soviet Russia into a vast prison camp.

The importance of ideology was one of the major themes of Solzhenitsyn's
epoch-making work. He made this clear by comparing tsarist with Soviet
repressions. The "Decembrist" prisoners in Nerchinsk? They had a norm of
118 pounds of ore to mine and load each day (and they were actually guilty
of crimes), "whereas Shalamov on the Kolyma had a work norm per day of
28,800 pounds."[41] Nineteenth-century revolutionaries risked only themselves,
not members of their families, who were left untouched.

What of the tsarist prisoners on Sakhalin Island of whom Anton Chekhov
spoke? Each day they received 56 ounces of bread, 14 ounces of meat, and 8-¾
ounces of cereal. In the GULag, prisoners would be envied if they received 24-½
ounces of soggy, dirty bread. "Among the Sakhalin officials Chekhov met clever,

energetic men, with scholarly leanings, who had studied the locality and local life thoroughly, and who had in fact written geographical and ethnographical studies. But even for a laugh it is impossible to imagine one such camp keeper in the whole Archipelago!"[42]

Solzhenitsyn was only warming to his theme. What happened to Pushkin, he asked, when the great writer told Nicholas I to his face that he sympathized with the Decembrists? He was told to go home, while "*our* Pushkins had heavy sentences slapped on them, went to the camps, and died." Or what about Vera Zasulich, the revolutionary who shot and almost killed Fyodor Trepov, chief of the St. Petersburg police force? A jury acquitted her! Seven attempts were made on the life of Tsar Alexander II. "What did he do about it? Ruin and banish half Petersburg, as happened after [Sergei] Kirov's murder? You know very well that such a thing could never enter his head."[43] Conclusion: "It was safer to keep dynamite during the rule of Alexander II than it was to shelter the orphan of an enemy of the people under Stalin."[44]

And what of the fate of Lenin, whose brother was executed for planning to assassinate Alexander III? He was admitted to law school at the University of Kazan. To be sure, he was subsequently expelled—for organizing an antigovernment demonstration. Was he shot? No, he was banished—to the family estate, where he intended to spend the summer anyway. Never did the tsarist government treat him in anything like the manner in which he was later to treat those whom he identified as enemies.

Solzhenitsyn rehearsed the early history of the Soviet regime, with its persecutions—especially of the church—its trials of opponents, real and imagined, and its choice of Solovki as the "first camp of the GULag."[45] He exhibited knowledge, gained by experience, of the means by which prisoners were transported from prison to prison, transit prison to labor camp, forced-labor camp to forced-labor camp. From experience, too, he told how the regime set common criminals, "revolutionary" in their own way, loose on "politicals," whom it judged to be far more dangerous. Most important, he pointed out that time in the GULag changed a man forever. "At home they continued to remember him as he had been, but he would never be that person again."[46]

In the chapter "The Archipelago Metastasizes," Solzhenitsyn described how the empire of the camps spread from Solovki throughout the Soviet Union. He also introduced one of that empire's key figures—Naftaly Aronovich Frenkel, a Turkish Jew who rose from prisoner to guard to powerful Archipelago functionary. Among the many ideas attributed to him was the assignment of food rations on the basis of the amount of work completed. In recognition of his abilities, Stalin appointed him chief of construction on the vast White Sea–Baltic (*Belomor*) canal project, which would link the White Sea with Lake Onega and provide access to the Baltic Sea. It was to be completed, without benefit of tractors, cranes, or earthmoving equipment, within twenty months.

Over 100,000 men (including Dmitry Likhachev, transferred from Solovki) slaved away with picks, shovels, sledgehammers, and handmade wheelbarrows, and yet, according to official reports, not a single one of them died! "Probably," Solzhenitsyn reasoned sarcastically, "They calculated it this way: One hundred thousand started the canal and one hundred thousand finished. And that meant they were all alive. They simply forgot about the prisoner transports devoured by the construction in the course of two fierce winters."[47] The best estimate of the death toll is 25,000, and in the end the canal was not deep or wide enough to be of significant use.

The White Sea–Baltic Canal was far from being the only mammoth project dreamed up by Stalin; there were other canals, railroads, highways, hydroelectric stations, ports, pipelines, and cities (including Magadan, capital of Kolyma). And as a result—more, a great many more, arrests. "The labor of the *zeks* was needed for degrading and particularly heavy work, which no one, under socialism, would wish to perform." The failure of many projects had little to do with the efforts of the *zeks* and almost everything to do with the often savage weather conditions, the lack of twentieth-century equipment, and the stunning (and amusing, if one were not a *zek*) incompetence of those in charge. Consider the railroad from Salekhard to Igarka, begun in 1949. "It all turned out to be superfluous," Solzhenitsyn wrote. "There was nothing there to be hauled on it. And they abandoned it too. But then one quails to say *whose* mistake that was. It was, after all, His Own," that is, Stalin's.[48]

Why, Solzhenitsyn asked rhetorically, did he and the millions of other *zeks* not, finally, rebel? For one thing, they had limited means at their disposal. He named the only possible four: protest; hunger strike; escape; and mutiny. For the first two to be effective there had to exist public opinion *outside* the camps—and there did not. Escape was nearly impossible and ultimately depended upon the attitude of the population. "And our population was *afraid* to help escapers [they could get twenty-five years], or even *betrayed* them, for mercenary or ideological reasons."[49]

But camp mutinies there were, and Solzhenitsyn was determined to sustain their memory. They began with the killing of traitors and informers—a form of terrorism, as he admitted; evil generates evil. But critics with whom he agreed in principle should, he insisted, imagine themselves in the position of *zeks*.

> If you ever get twenty-five years for nothing, if you find yourself wearing four number patches on your clothes, holding your hands permanently behind your back, submitting to searches morning and evening, working until you are utterly exhausted, dragged into the cooler whenever someone denounces you, trodden deeper and deeper into the ground—from the hole you're in, the fine words of the great humanists will sound like the chatter of the well-fed and free.[50]

A mood of rebellion was growing among *zeks*. In Ekibastuz, Solzhenitsyn's camp, they refused to work and went on a hunger strike early in 1952. "Our bellies were empty, our hearts were in our boots," he wrote, "but some higher need was being satisfied."[51] That was not nothing, but after a few days of resistance the *zeks* failed to achieve much more.

The Kengir (Kazakhstan) uprising of May–June 1954, which Solzhenitsyn also described, lasted forty days. Emboldened by the fall and execution of Beria, the *zeks* were not prepared to stand idly by after guards murdered some of their number. They refused to report for work but soon gave in to force and better food. But then the authorities made a mistake—they introduced common prisoners into the politicals' camp. By this action, Solzhenitsyn wrote, "the bosses obtained not a pacified camp but the biggest mutiny in the history of the GULag Archipelago."[52]

Threatened by the suddenly aggressive politicals, the "thieves" decided to join forces against the bosses; they began the revolt and were its first casualties. As planned, the politicals then acted in support of their unwonted comrades. A delegation of authorities, including generals from Moscow, attempted to quiet things down by promising reforms. Soon, however, it became clear to the *zeks* that the bosses were playing for time, and they took control of the camp, elected a negotiating commission, set up a provisional "government," and fortified their position. *Zek* negotiators demanded punishment for guards guilty of murder, the removal of locks from hut doors, an eight-hour work day, unrestricted correspondence with relatives, and a review of prisoners' cases.

The *zeks* reveled in their freedom, including fraternization with the women prisoners, but few of them could have believed that they could prevail against a brutal and determined force. "The believers," Solzhenitsyn wrote, "prayed, and leaving the outcome of the Kengir revolt in God's hands, were as always the calmest of people." On June 22, as the regime prepared to crush the revolt, "outside radio announced that the prisoners' demands had been accepted! A member of the Presidium of the Central Committee was on his way!"[53] At 3:30 a.m. on June 26, Soviet armed forces launched a massive assault that claimed as many as five hundred lives.

Solzhenitsyn described *The GULag Archipelago* as "a call to repentance," his own and his country's.[54] In other words, it had, before anything else, a spiritual purpose. That and his growing political conservatism alienated many who had initially rallied to his support. "I simply did not realize that the support I received from 'progressive society' was but a passing phase based on a misunderstanding."[55]

Although he knew, for example, that Tvardovsky had the highest regard for his talent and considered him to be a friend, Solzhenitsyn also knew that the famed editor was a true believer in Marxism, who despised the Orthodox Church. "Atheism too ... was a sincerely held belief congenial to everyone on the *Novy Mir* editorial board, including, alas, Tvardovsky."[56] Solzhenitsyn never forgot the debt he owed Tvardovsky for championing him, but as the years passed their different views of life and the world drove them further and further apart. The same may be said of Solzhenitsyn's friendship with Lev Kopelev.

Lyusha Chukovskaya was put off by Solzhenitsyn's patriotism and Orthodoxy and flatly refused to type his letter to Patriarch Pimen, apparently because she did not wish the Church to stiffen its backbone and play a serious role in public life. Veniamin Teush remained a Bolshevik at heart. Mirra Petrova was a literary historian and critic who served Solzhenitsyn as something of a research assistant, particularly with respect to prerevolutionary Russia, but as she read the manuscript copy of *The Red Wheel*, the huge novelistic history of which more in due course, she was horrified by its conservatism. "It was," Solzhenitsyn later recalled, "with particular irritation—almost personal pique—that she objected to chapters with a religious theme."[57]

Far better known than any of these "invisible allies," was Andrei Dmitrievich Sakharov, Solzhenitsyn's only rival for preeminence among Soviet "dissidents." No former *zek*, Sakharov was a leading nuclear physicist (he helped father the H-bomb), three-time Hero of Socialist Labor, and winner of Stalin and

Lenin Prizes. But his conscience began to trouble him with respect to nuclear testing and, once having awakened, led to his step by step disenchantment with Soviet rule. Solzhenitsyn met him at the end of August 1968, just after the Soviet occupation of Czechoslovakia and shortly after the appearance, in *samizdat*, of the brilliant scientist's memorandum "Progress, Coexistence, and Intellectual Freedom."[58]

In that rather scattershot program, Sakharov called attention to the threat of nuclear war and denounced Stalinism but continued to hold up socialism as a moral ideal that had to its credit many practical successes. "The views of the present author are," he wrote, "profoundly socialist"—and so they were. He placed his hope for a peaceful coexistence between the Soviet Union and the West on a "convergence" of their respective political and social systems brought about through the efforts of anti-Stalinist reformers in the former and leftist reformers in the latter.

Although he formed a favorable impression of Sakharov as a human being, Solzhenitsyn told him that "any kind of convergence was out of the question. The West was caught up in materialism and permissiveness, and socialism might prove to be its final ruin." He remained cool toward the technological progress that Sakharov advocated and instead emphasized the importance of "an underlying spiritual goal" in the struggle against the Soviet regime,[59] an idea that was alien to Sakharov, a good and courageous man but one who confessed no religious belief. "Philosophically," he said, "I am a liberal and a humanist."[60] With such a man, Solzhenitsyn could never forge a close relationship.

And then there was Natalya, his wife. She hated *The GULag Archipelago* because Solzhenitsyn was working on it at his summer dacha near Rozhdestvo-on-the-Istya or at Haava in Estonia—anywhere but with her in Ryazan. There is no doubt that he placed his writing before his marriage and that that was a primary source of alienation. "If only I could carry on with my work uninterrupted," he told Michael Scammell. "If only we could arrange it so that private matters didn't get in the way of work."[61] By the late sixties, all hope of saving the marriage had gone; driven to despair, Natalya attempted to take her own life.

Having survived the attempt, she exacted what revenge she could by penning an accusatory memoir of the marriage: *Sanya: My Life with Aleksandr Solzhenitsyn* (published in Russian, 1974, by the Novosti Press Agency). In it she wrote, among other unflattering things, that "the central purpose of *Archipelago*, as I saw it in the process of creation, was not to portray the life of the country or even to depict daily life in a camp, but, rather, to present a collection of camp folklore."[62] By the time the book appeared, Solzhenitsyn had obtained a divorce, clearing the way for his marriage to Natalya Svetlova (called Alya), a divorcée and mathematician who had already presented him with two children.

Solzhenitsyn met Alya, more than twenty years his junior, in 1968, a week after the Soviet army wrote an end to the "Prague Spring." So impressed was he that he involved her in his work immediately. She quickly became the most important of those who sympathized with his beliefs and view of the world. "I had dreamed in vain," he wrote in *Invisible Allies*, "of finding a male friend whose ideas would be as close to my own as were those that Natasha [Alya] now came out with unprompted.... There was no gap at all in our fundamental convictions."[63] In 1969 he transferred his most complete archive from Nikolai Kobozev to Alya's care.

Alya was to remain the central figure in Solzhenitsyn's life, but as his outlook on life and the world came into ever sharper focus, he found others for whom he had an elective affinity; one of them was the great cellist, Mstislav Rostropovich. In November 1967 Rostropovich played two concerts in Ryazan and sought out Solzhenitsyn, who had been in the audience for one of them. They talked for several hours and formed an immediate friendship. Two years later, Rostropovich offered Solzhenitsyn a flat in his dacha—one hundred meters from Sakharov's dacha—in Zhukovka, an attractive settlement southwest of Moscow. "This refuge," Solzhenitsyn wrote in his memoirs, "was the biggest present I remember ever receiving."[64]

It was a generosity for which the KGB would make Rostropovich pay dearly; he was banned from foreign tours, then from performing and conducting, and finally, in 1974, forced to leave the country. And yet, like Solzhenitsyn, he refused to be broken. As one of his students has recalled, "Religion had become of increasing importance in his life, for it gave him the spiritual strength to remain steadfast in his resolve to live by his conscience and not to compromise himself."[65]

Solzhenitsyn's friendship with Nikita Struve began as a professional relationship. He was in search of a Russian-language publisher in the West, and Struve's Paris-based YMCA Press was an obvious choice. Thanks to financial support from the YMCA, the press was a going concern and specialized in philosophy and religion; it was the principal outlet for Russian intellectuals living abroad. Even before they met, Solzhenitsyn knew Struve by name—his grandfather was Pyotr (Peter) Struve, who had begun his career as a moderate Marxist but came to reject every form of socialism in favor of a conservative liberalism. A sincerely religious man, Struve was an important contributor to *Vekhi* (*Landmarks*).

In his *Landmarks* essay, "The Intelligentsia and Revolution," Pyotr Struve argued that the Russian intelligentsia, rightly understood, was born under the sign of atheistic socialism. Earlier critics of tsarist rule such as Nikolai Novikov and Aleksandr Radishchev, both of whom ran afoul of Catherine the Great, belonged to Russia's educated classes and maintained religious beliefs—they were different spiritual types than atheists such as Mikhail Bakunin and Nikolai Chernyshevsky. Unlike other of his fellow contributors, Struve could discern nothing "religious" in atheistic socialism. From a truly religious standpoint, he insisted, it is inner perfection that matters; "the problem of life's external organization is something secondary."[66]

Nikita Struve was a "torchbearer for Russian culture."[67] "We believe that Russia is marked out as God's elect," he wrote to a friend. "It is the only great country in which the Orthodox religion survives and Orthodoxy embodies truth and life in all their fullness." This was music to Solzhenitsyn's ears. In the early 1970s he began what was to become a close collaboration, "both as publisher and as friend."[68]

Struve belonged to that remarkable circle of exiled Russian intellectuals who settled in Paris. It included Nikolai Berdyaev but also Sergei Bulgakov, for whom Solzhenitsyn had a high regard. Born in 1871, Bulgakov was the son of an Orthodox priest. He himself attended, but did not graduate from, seminary in Orel, where he lost his faith, became a Marxist, and turned his attention to political economy. But under the influence of Dostoevsky, the religious philosopher Vladimir Soloviev, and his profound love of nature, he regained his faith in his thirtieth year.

In 1906 Bulgakov published a long journal article (later reprinted as a short book) entitled "Karl Marx as a Religious Type." In it, Solzhenitsyn observed, the author showed "that atheism is the chief inspirational and emotional hub of Marxism and that all the rest of the doctrine has simply been tacked on."[69] According to Bulgakov, Marx was, before all else, a zealous atheist. "In Marx's militant atheism," he wrote, "one can see the central nerve of his entire life-work, one of its main stimuli."[70] This atheistic humanism was, he argued, itself a form of religion—an ultimate conviction that gave meaning and direction to Marx's life.

ntance and a willingness to forgive others must precede one's own
and, according to Solzhenitsyn, Russians (including himself) had
ich to repent, as individuals and as a nation—and not only for the
oviet period. There were, for example, the terrible persecutions of
vers, for whom Solzhenitsyn expressed considerable sympathy, and
tal serfdom of the Petersburg period (early eighteenth century to
contemporary Russians were not alive at the time of many national
st, but "the nation is mystically welded together in a community of
inescapable destiny is common repentance."[83]

ce led to forgiveness and to a turn away from sinful ways; it cre-
osphere for self-limitation" and thus for true freedom. "After the
l of unlimited freedom, after the Marxist concept of freedom as
f the yoke of necessity—here is the true Christian definition of free-
m is *self-restriction*! Restriction of the self for the sake of others!"[84]
for individuals *and* for nations.

yn had no use for the idea of infinite progress, which he viewed
nnected with unlimited freedom. For him a stable economy was
e than one of endless growth. He thought the space race pointless
remained to be done to make life in Russia's villages more livable.
perial adventures, he advocated the development of Russia's great
h national self-limitation could lead to Russia's renewal.

r, Igor Shafarevich, contributed three essays to *From Under the*
hematician of world renown and an Orthodox Christian, he and
met early in 1968. According to the latter, "Shafarevich was from
ly tied to Russia, the land and its history: they are one flesh, with
odstream, a single heartbeat."[85] The most important of Shafarev-
s "Socialism in Our Past and Future," a précis of *The Socialist*
published by the YMCA Press in 1975; the book is one of the
f socialism ever written.

hafarevich argued, is not a phenomenon of the last two cen-
form, it can be found in the ancient, medieval, and modern
it merely an economic system; its fundamental aims include the
ivate property, the abolition of religion, the destruction of the
destruction of hierarchy (that is the demand for equality, under-
y). Shafarevich traced socialism back to Plato and the Gnostic

A similar insight informed Bulgakov's assessment of the Russian intelligentsia in *Vekhi*. The members of that guild, he argued there, adopted, with a fervor
that could only be described as religious, the atheism and materialism of the
Enlightenment. "Atheism," he wrote, "is the common faith into which are baptized all who enter the bosom of the humanistic intelligentsia church." He called
attention to the *intelligent*'s dogmatism, self-worship, and faith in science and
"progress"—his (and her) loss of any sense of personal responsibility. "Extremely
unpopular among the intelligentsia are the concepts of *personal* morality, *personal* self-improvement, and the development of the *individual* (and, vice-versa,
the word *social* has a special, sacramental character)."[71] Not they themselves, but
"society" was in need of rebirth.

In 1917 Bulgakov received a professorial appointment at Moscow University
and the following year was ordained priest, an event witnessed by Berdyaev,
Pyotr Struve, and Fr. Pavel Florensky. In 1919 he fled to the Crimea before being
driven into exile in 1923. He settled initially in Prague, but in 1925 he moved
to Paris, became active in the ecumenical movement, and helped to establish
the St. Sergius Orthodox Theological Institute, which he served as dean until
his death in 1944. The institute was the main intellectual center of the Russian
Orthodox Church in exile and a key point of contact between Orthodoxy
and Western Christians. It trained such important Orthodox thinkers as Frs.
Alexander Schmemann and John Meyendorff, both of whom were to continue
the St. Sergius tradition at St. Vladimir's Orthodox Theological Seminary in
Crestwood, New York.

In 1974, Nikita Struve published a collection of essays under the title *Iz pod
glyb* (translated into English as *From Under the Rubble*). Solzhenitsyn was the
guiding force behind the collaborative work, which he modeled on *Vekhi*. In
"The Smatterers," one of his three contributions, he wrote that "even after sixty
years its testimony has not lost its brightness: *Vekhi* today still seems to us to
have been a vision of the future"—that of a Russian intelligentsia defined by its
ideology, which was atheistic and revolutionary. It was precisely the intelligentsia's repudiation of religious morality, Solzhenitsyn charged, that "supplied an
easy justification both for the hastily constituted revolutionary tribunals and the
rough justice meted out in the cellars of the Cheka."[72]

Vekhi contributors could not foresee the terror to come, but they knew that
nothing so enraged members of the intelligentsia as much as religious belief.

What they prized in Gogol "was his denunciation of the state system and the ruling classes. But the moment he embarked upon the spiritual quest that was dearest of all to him he was flayed by the journalistic press and excommunicated from progressive society." As for Dostoevsky, he "was altogether detested by the intelligentsia."[73]

By the 1970s, Solzhenitsyn observed, those who passed for members of the intelligentsia were little more than "smatterers," semi-educated individuals who lacked any conviction and sought only to advance or protect their careers. Cynical with respect to the official ideology, they were prepared at all times to give lip service to the lie. In this they were even more repugnant than the pre-revolutionary intelligentsia. And yet, not all was lost. Thanks in part to those who collaborated with him on *From Under the Rubble*, Solzhenitsyn held out hope for the formation of a new intelligentsia, or as he preferred a "*sacrificial elite*," the members of which were willing to pay the price for refusing to say in public what they did not believe and in fact ridiculed in private.

"Our present system," Solzhenitsyn wrote in "As Breathing and Consciousness Return," another contribution to *From Under the Rubble*, "is unique in world history, because over and above its physical and economic constraints, it demands of us total surrender of our souls, continuous and active participation in the general, conscious *lie*."[74] A refusal by enough of his countrymen to continue participation would constitute a moral revolution—and for Solzhenitsyn moral, *inner* revolutions were far more important than political, *outer* revolutions.

By the same token, he regarded inner freedom as more important than outer freedom, or what one usually refers to as "liberty." There is, he insisted, "a miscalculation in the urgent pursuit of political freedom as the first and main thing: we should first have a clear idea of what to do with it."[75] This echoes the judgment of Edmund Burke: "The effect of liberty to individuals is, that they may do what they please: We ought to see what it will please them to do, before we risque congratulations, which may be soon turned into complaints."[76]

For Solzhenitsyn real change could take place only in the hearts of men, in their moral character. That, not "happiness," was the true aim of life. The form of the political state was no more than of secondary significance. He never for a moment believed that "democracy," particularly as understood in the West, was the *only*, much less the best, form of government. In this regard too he would have agreed with Burke, who asked: "Is it then a truth so universally acknowledged, that a pure democracy is the only tolerable form into which human society can be thrown, that a man is not permitted to hesitate

---

about its merits, without the suspicion of being a foe to mankind?"[77]

In fact, Solzhenitsyn had a good bit of government, as long as they were n nature. Russia (and not Russia alone) ha under various forms of authoritarian rul functioned for centuries on end in many provided certain limits are not exceeded life, as much as any democratic republic tems were stability, continuity, and imm there were dangers, the greatest of which resisting any change.

This was more likely in secular er ages, though their power was ostensibly before God and their own consciences. gerous precisely because it is difficult t them."[79] Nothing, he knew, bound H Union it was not simply a matter of S an ideology and a system. As Martin Soviet experiment turned totalitarian it was socialist."[80]

Solzhenitsyn made that clear in "A which was his formal response to Intellectual Freedom." He praised the that, since 1956, it was relatively safe all of the dissidents of the 1960s, st cows. They shrank from admitting th faithful—if also very untalented—he one reason why Solzhenitsyn always

Solzhenitsyn also criticized Sakha ognize the nation's need of repentan on the day of forgiveness, and ask to one of the most important day Sunday, the day before the beginni Parishioners make a prostration (t the priest (and in some parishes, be ness. The priest responds "God for[ ]

---

forgiveness
much of wh
sins of the S
the Old Beli
the often br
1917). True,
sins of the p
guilt, and its

Repentan
ated "the atm
Western ide
acceptance o
dom. Freedo
This was true

Solzhenits
as closely co
more desirab
when so mud
Instead of im
northeast. Su

Another write
Rubble. A mat
Solzhenitsyn
birth insepara
a common blo
ich's essays w
Phenomenon,
finest studies

Socialism,
turies; in som
worlds. Nor is
abolition of pr
family, and the
stood as *identi*

and Manichean sects, and pointed to the socialist tendencies of many of the heretical movements of the Middle Ages—Cathars, Waldensians, and Taborites (radical Hussites). Like socialist ideology, these movements were "imbued with the notion of a coming fundamental break, of the end and destruction of the old world and the beginning of a new order."[86]

The new order was invariably characterized by the common ownership of property and usually by sexual "liberation" and state (as opposed to family) rearing of children. These appealed to latter-day socialists because they combined religious passion with hatred of orthodox (in the West, Catholic) Christianity. But with the coming of the Renaissance, socialist ideology "threw off its mystical and religious form and based itself on a materialistic and rationalist view of the world"; it became atheistic.[87]

Socialism's atheism became more pronounced before and during the Enlightenment. Shafarevich called particular attention to the bizarre figure of Jean Meslier (1664–1729), a priest of the Catholic Church who served a parish at Étrépigny in Champagne for some forty years, before taking his own life at age sixty-five. He left behind a long *Testament*, which Voltaire found to be rewarding—in 1762 he published an expurgated and tendentiously edited version entitled *Extraits des sentiments de Jean Meslier*. Meslier's two driving passions were hatred of religion, and of the person of Christ in particular—he was an atheist throughout his years as a priest—and of inequality. "I am reminded," Meslier wrote, "of the wish of one man who expressed the desire that 'all the mighty of this world and the noble lords be hanged and strangled with loops made of priests' bowels.'"[88]

Like all those attracted to socialism, Meslier was a fanatical egalitarian, a kind of Shigalyov—from Dostoevsky's *The Devils*. Shafarevich cited Peter Verkhovensky's description of Shigalyovism:

> The thirst for education is already an aristocratic thirst. As soon as there is a family or love, there is a desire for property. We shall throttle that desire: we shall unleash drunkenness, scandal, denunciations; we shall unleash unprecedented debauchery; we shall extinguish every genius in his infancy. Everything must be reduced to the common denominator, total equality.... Each belongs to all, and all to each. All are slaves and equal in slavery. In extreme cases it will mean defamation and murder, but the main thing is equality. First there will be a drop in the standard of education, in learning and talent. A high level of learning and talent is accessible only to the very brainy. We must abolish the brainy! The brainy have

always seized power and been despots and have always brought more debauchery than good. We will execute or exile them. We will cut out Cicero's tongue, gouge out Copernicus's eyes, stone Shakespeare to death—that's Shigalyovism![89]

This is the nihilistic logic of radical egalitarianism—and of utopianism. In fact, Shafarevich argued that the urge for destruction of the existing world, and subconsciously for individual self-destruction (often seen in revolutionaries who seek martyrdom or complete submission to the movement), was rooted in *Thanatos*, the death instinct. Had he written his book a decade later he could have presented, as evidence, the socialists' commitment to abortion and euthanasia.

From Alya, Rostropovich, and his fellow contributors to *From Under the Rubble*, Solzhenitsyn was able to draw added strength to continue his duel with Andropov, who saw to it that he was expelled from the Writers' Union on November 4, 1969. But almost one year later (October 1970), the Swedish Academy awarded Solzhenitsyn the Nobel Prize for Literature "for the ethical force with which he has pursued the indispensable traditions of Russian literature." Andropov was beside himself, and the Politburo hastened to send instructions to the Soviet Ambassador in Stockholm: "Visit Mr. T. Nilsson, Minister of Foreign Affairs of Sweden, and announce to him the following: Both Soviet literary circles and the Soviet public at large consider the decision of the Swedish Academy to award the Nobel Prize to Solzhenitsyn as an unfriendly act with respect to the Soviet Union and are filled with indignation."[90]

Solzhenitsyn knew that if he traveled to Sweden to accept his prize Andropov would see to it that he would not be allowed to return—he therefore decided against the trip. Disappointed, Andropov knew that, because of the prize, he would find it more difficult—though not impossible—to take action against his prey; moreover, he worried that Soviet citizens would also know. In a memorandum dated March 27, 1972, therefore, he posed the regime's alternatives: "In this situation the issue arises either of criminally prosecuting Solzhenitsyn or expelling him from Soviet territory. It would appear expedient to select the latter course of action."[91]

Solzhenitsyn continued to work on his writing projects, but in August 1973 he set them aside and on pure impulse drafted a *Letter to the Soviet Leaders*; on

September 5 he sent one copy, in secrecy, to Leonid Brezhnev. It was an appeal not to an enemy but to a countryman. Could the Soviet leader not see that it was *ideology*, the Progressive World View, that led the regime to act in ways contrary to the interests of Russia and her people? Even Stalin, during the Second World War, recognized this. "He wisely discarded [Marxist ideology], all but ceased to mention it and unfurled instead the old Russian banner—sometimes, indeed, the standard of Orthodoxy—and we conquered!"[92]

Solzhenitsyn hastened to add that he did not expect the Soviet leaders to step down and establish a democracy—the country was not prepared for such a sudden and dramatic change of government. In any event, authoritarianism was not the problem. It was "the ideological lies that are daily foisted upon us. Not so much authoritarianism as arbitrariness and illegality." For a thousand years Russia lived with an authoritarian order, "one that possessed a strong moral foundation, embryonic and rudimentary though it was—not the ideology of universal violence, but Christian Orthodoxy." He himself, he told Brezhnev, believed that Christianity was "the only living spiritual force capable of undertaking the spiritual healing of Russia. But I request and propose no special privileges for it, simply that it should be treated fairly and not suppressed."[93]

It is difficult to believe that Solzhenitsyn held out much hope that his letter would sway Brezhnev—and of course it did not. At a Politburo meeting the Soviet leader reported that he had "received Solzhenitsyn's letter to the Central Committee addressed to me. He writes in a slightly different manner compared to his previous letters but it's still nonsense."[94]

In the same month that Solzhenitsyn was drafting his letter, Andropov informed the Politburo that the KGB had obtained a copy of *The GULag Archipelago*—following a brutal interrogation of Elizaveta Voronyanskaya, to whom Solzhenitsyn had entrusted it; the distraught woman subsequently hanged herself (according to Andropov). Fortunately, Solzhenitsyn had sent a copy to the West, and when he heard of the KGB seizure, he instructed the YMCA Press to publish it immediately. The first volume appeared in late December—not, as he had requested, on January 7, Orthodox Christmas (his habit was to schedule important moves for feast days in the Orthodox Church).

Not being concerned with Christmas, members of the Politburo met on January 7 and decided to bring Solzhenitsyn to trial for slandering the Soviet

Union and defiling "the blessed memory of V. I. Lenin."[95] Exactly one month later, however, Andropov sent a memorandum to the Central Committee, informing it that Chancellor Willy Brandt, speaking in Munich, had indicated that Solzhenitsyn would be welcome to reside and work in West Germany; he therefore favored stripping Solzhenitsyn of Soviet citizenship and expelling him from the country. On February 12, without warning, Solzhenitsyn was arrested and the following day put on a plane to Frankfurt am Main, and what would be twenty years of exile in the West.

CHAPTER FOUR

IN THE WEST

From the Frankfurt airport a Foreign Ministry Mercedes sped Solzhenitsyn to the hamlet of Langenbroich (in the Eifel hills west of Bonn) and the home of Nobel Prize winner Heinrich Böll, who had visited and secretly aided Solzhenitsyn during trips to the Soviet Union. Despite the German author's hospitality, however, the new exile was eager to find a home and return to work. He liked the Germans and admired traditional Germany, but he never gave serious consideration to settling there.[1] Norway's climate and way of life appealed, but the obscurity of its language did not. Solzhenitsyn therefore decided to scout out Switzerland, especially Zurich, home to his lawyer Fritz Heeb, a lifelong socialist from whom he eventually distanced himself. More important, the city was Lenin's most famous place of exile. It would make possible a greater "feel" for the Bolshevik chieftain's life in the years leading up to the Revolution.

Zurich it was to be—but only for the time being. When asked at a press conference why he lived in Switzerland, Solzhenitsyn replied: "I do not live in Switzerland, I live in Russia. All my interests, all the things I care about, are in Russia."[2] In March Solzhenitsyn was joined by Alya, who, along with the children, brought with her his library and archive. The city's mayor had found for the family a villa near the city center and offered as a quiet work place his farmhouse in a mountain village. It was all quite provisional, but Solzhenitsyn found Swiss democracy to his liking—small, local, and participatory. He was particularly impressed by the canton of Appenzell; if only, he mused, the leaders of the Great Powers would take their inspiration from its political life![3]

Mass democracies were, in Solzhenitsyn's view, a different matter, something that soon began to dawn on his Western admirers, for whom democracy was the *only* legitimate form of government. In March the YMCA Press published the

Letter to the Soviet Leaders, and it was quickly translated; those who read it were made angrily aware that its author was not another Sakharov, who described the *Letter* as "potentially dangerous" and who never, in Solzhenitsyn's view, "took to heart the cause of [Russia's] national rebirth."[4]

Nor was Solzhenitsyn a secular figure. The Western left was appalled to discover that he was not merely a nominal Christian. He was quick, for example, to honor a request from Metropolitan Philaret of the Russian Orthodox Church Abroad (or Russian Orthodox Church Outside of Russia—ROCOR). Founded in Serbia in 1922, ROCOR was the most conservative of Orthodox jurisdictions (it regarded the Moscow patriarchate as compromised, and many of its leaders were monarchists). The metropolitan asked Solzhenitsyn what he and his faithful might do to render assistance to cobelievers in Russia. In response, Solzhenitsyn published an open letter, dated August 1974, in the September 27 issue of *Novoe Russkoe Slovo.*

The metropolitan may have regretted his request for, as always, Solzhenitsyn gave his opinion without worrying that he might give offense. In general he did not have a favorable view of the church hierarchy, in Russia or abroad. For the faith and courage of humble parish priests and the Russian people, however, he expressed nothing but admiration. He criticized the disunity that marked the history of the Russian Orthodox churches abroad, having primarily in mind the rivalry and sometimes open hostility between ROCOR and the Orthodox Church in America (OCA). "The only correct path," he concluded, "is the one leading to the merger of all branches of the Russian Church."[5]

While he was at it, Solzhenitsyn called attention to what, in his view, was an even worse sin of disunity, that which separated the Russian Orthodox Church (at home and abroad) from the Old Believers, those who, following Archpriest Avvakum, refused to accept the seventeenth-century reforms (ritual and textual) imposed by Patriarch Nikon, reforms—among them the destruction of icons judged to depart from ancient Greek models and the making of the sign of the cross with three, rather than two, fingers—aimed at achieving uniformity between Russian and Greek Orthodox practices but which, in the eyes of resisters, had the effect of mutilating the very vehicle of men's salvation.[6] The Church, backed by the state, persecuted the resisters, whom they referred to disdainfully as *raskolniki* (schismatics).

The Old Believers were "subjected to terrible corporal punishment, such as having a tongue cut out, being burnt at the stake [as was Avvakum], or, in the most horrible instance, being smoked alive 'like bacon.'"[7] (Nikon carried the day but ran afoul of Tsar Alexis, whose power he hoped to equal, and of fellow patriarchs. At the Great Moscow Sobor, or Synod, of 1666–1667, Paisios, Patriarch of Alexandria, and Makarios, Patriarch of Antioch, deposed him, defrocked him as a priest, and reduced him to the status of a simple monk.[8])

> I cannot bring myself [Solzhenitsyn wrote] to call these sturdy, faithful, ancient-orthodox Christians by a name like "schismatic." I avoid even calling them Old Believers, for in that case what are we but New Believers. Simply because they did not possess sufficient spiritual agility to accept the hasty and dubious recommendations of those who had visited the Greek patriarchs, because they retained the practice of crossing themselves with two fingers, the means by which our whole church of the seven capitals made the sign of the cross, because of these things we condemned them to punishments just as harsh as those dealt us by atheists under Lenin and Stalin. And yet our hearts have never quivered with repentance![9]

There were many reasons for Solzhenitsyn's defense of the Old Believers, including their political conservatism, opposition to Western influence, and readiness to flee the "permissiveness, disorder, and lack of religious piety that they encountered in densely populated [that is, urban] areas."[10] At the same time, he had to overlook the facts that they bore a resemblance to radical Protestant sects, that Chernyshevsky had defended them as rebels against authority, and that Dostoevsky had named the murderer in *Crime and Punishment* "Raskolnikov."

Two months after his open letter to ROCOR appeared, Solzhenitsyn traveled to Stockholm to be recognized in person as a Nobel Laureate. That was one of the many destinations he scheduled in an effort to gain a better understanding of the West and to awaken Westerners to the ongoing Soviet threat. In April 1975 he visited Paris, where he was heralded as a great and prophetic writer. Next on his itinerary was Canada, where he looked for a more secluded place of residence. From the eastern part of that vast land, he and Alya traveled westward to British Columbia and thence to Alaska, which appealed because of its harsh climate and its history as a former Russian possession.

But there was something more important. It was in Alaska that the Russian Orthodox first evangelized the native populations of North America. In the company of Gregory, the Russian-born Bishop of Sitka and Alaska, Solzhenitsyn visited Sitka (New Archangel), where St. Innocent of Alaska (Ivan

Popov-Veniaminov, 1797–1879) brought the Orthodox faith to the Tlingit people. To Solzhenitsyn's delight, Christian Tlingits inducted him into their clan.[11]

Moving south, Solzhenitsyn visited the Hoover Institution on War, Revolution and Peace, which houses a rich collection of papers and documents on twentieth-century Russian history; the Institution made him an honorary fellow. From Stanford he traveled to Oregon to visit a community of Old Believers—a branch of Belaya Krinitsa (a monastery in Bukovina) faithful to the hierarchical tradition; they had, that is, priests and bishops.

On June 30 Solzhenitsyn was in Washington, DC, to speak to members of the AFL-CIO. (He and Alya had limited time for sightseeing, but they did attend a concert, with Rostropovich conducting, at the Kennedy Center.) After being introduced by George Meany, Solzhenitsyn quickly won the union members over. He himself, he said truthfully, had spent many years as a bricklayer and foundry man. And he praised a worker-martyr of whom they had never heard: Aleksandr Shlyapnikov. A metalworker and communist, Shlyapnikov led the so-called "Workers' Opposition" to Soviet policies in the early 1920s. Arrested in 1935, he refused to implicate others and was executed in 1937.

In words that echoed George Kennan's theory of containment, Solzhenitsyn told the gathered workers that Soviet leaders respected only firmness and held in contempt those who constantly gave in to them. The message was much the same when, on July 9, he again addressed members of the AFL-CIO, this time in New York City. On that occasion, however, he added a dire warning about the direction of Western society. The West might soon be faced with a fate similar to that experienced by Russia. Westerners may say: "It will never happen here. This will never come to us. It is not possible here." But: "It can happen. It is possible. As a Russian proverb says: 'When it happens to you, you'll know it's true.'"[12]

Solzhenitsyn had a more favorable view of American workers than he did of the British. He arrived in England in February 1976, and on March 24 he delivered over the BBC a highly critical address to the British people. "I intend," he informed his audience, "to speak frankly and I shall not try to please you or to flatter you in any way." Nor did he. He reminded his listeners that England forced the repatriation of some 100,000 Soviet citizens at the conclusion of World War II—most of whom Stalin put to death. That unconscionable act, he said, "has left a deep and painful mark on the Russian memory."[13]

Solzhenitsyn was not finished. "At Nuremberg you [sat] amicably side by side with judges who were just as much murderers as those on trial."[14] He maintained that the British and Western elites exhibited an inexplicable sympathy for revolutionaries and terrorists and a contempt for any reference to spiritual regeneration. Like so many members of Russia's nineteenth-century intelligentsia they viewed socialism as "a kind of worldly religion," forgetting or not caring that socialism/equality demanded compulsion.

Finally, he expressed his regret that the West seemed unwilling to profit from Russia's historical experience. "We, the oppressed peoples of Russia, the oppressed peoples of Eastern Europe, watch with anguish the tragic enfeeblement of Europe. We offer you the experience of our suffering; we would like you to accept it without having to pay the monstrous price of death and slavery that we have paid."[15]

Solzhenitsyn had kinder words for Spain, his next stop. The country reminded him of Russia, not least in its extremes of faith and unbelief. He outraged the left—in Spain, in France (*Le Monde*), in Belgium (the International Confederation of Free Trade Unions)—by telling them that General Francisco Franco's government was far superior to that of the Soviet Union. Under his authoritarian—not totalitarian or fascist—rule, Spaniards could travel abroad freely, read newspapers from around the world, and criticize public policy. "If we had such conditions," he said, "we would be thunderstruck, we would say this was unprecedented freedom."[16] Needless to say, the world press, dominated by the left, subjected his remarks to relentless criticism. The brief honeymoon he had enjoyed in the West was over, and he decided to seek a more remote place to live and, in future, to let his books speak for him.

Solzhenitsyn's choice of a more permanent home fell on Vermont, where in 1975 he had been a guest of Norwich University. The property to which he and his family moved in September 1976 lay on the outskirts of the village of Cavendish. Fr. Alexis Vinogradov, a trained architect, designed (with Solzhenitsyn's help) the home and compound that was surrounded by an electric fence and possessed a complicated security system. An underground tunnel connected the main house to a tower, on the top floor of which Solzhenitsyn worked—standing up because of sciatica. There was a chapel dedicated to St. Sergius of Radonezh. On the lower floors were his books, printing facilities, and research documents.[17] All of this may seem to argue paranoia, but long years in the camps and under KGB surveillance make it understandable.

Solzhenitsyn rarely emerged from his compound, but in 1978 he accepted an invitation to deliver the commencement address at Harvard University. The thousands who braved inclement weather on June 8 were treated, if that is the word, to an unexpected and controversial indictment of the Western world. Having lived in that world for four years, the famous exile had formed an unblinking view of it. As much as he wished to see an end to the Soviet regime, he made it clear that he did not regard the West as a model for a post-communist Russia because "through deep suffering, people in our country have now achieved a spiritual development of such intensity that the Western system in its present state of spiritual exhaustion does not look attractive."[18]

So obsessed was the West with "human rights," Solzhenitsyn noted, that it had forgotten about human obligations. Its freedom had degenerated into license, its "media" filled minds and souls with gossip and nonsense, its popular culture served only to coarsen and degrade, its people exhibited an unthinking sympathy for socialism, and its excessive rationalism and philosophical materialism undermined the ability to recognize evil and destroyed the habit of spiritual reflection.

At the root of these signs of decline, Solzhenitsyn argued, was the "irreligious humanistic consciousness" and worship of Man that could be traced back to the Renaissance and the Enlightenment—that is, to the origins of modernity—and that envisioned no higher human aim than happiness. No wonder then that so many in the West were driven by hedonism and material gain. And like communists in the Soviet Union (communism being the most infamous child of modernity), Westerners "have placed too much hope in politics and social reforms, only to find out that [they] were being deprived of [their] most precious possession: [their] spiritual life."[19] On such a view, spiritual development, not happiness, was the proper aim of life.

The immediate reaction to the address was the predictable one of outrage. Critics described Solzhenitsyn, among other things, as "a Cold Warrior," "a fanatic," and "a furious doctrinaire."[20] An oft-repeated charge was that he misunderstood the West in general and America in particular. At the same time, his critics pretended to an expert knowledge of Russia. "His views," according to the *Washington Post*, "remain very Russian." To Mary McGrory the form of government Solzhenitsyn seemed to prefer "sounds czarist." According to her, Arthur Schlesinger, Jr. and others, he failed to appreciate America's "vibrant pluralistic society" and the "civilizing influences of a democratic tradition."[21]

Solzhenitsyn was not alone in being unimpressed by the "vibrant pluralistic society" and the "civilizing influences of a democratic tradition"; America's Founding Fathers had taken a dim view of democracy. After all the outrage, the most important question remained: was what the exiled writer said of the West true? According to the *Washington Star*, he "probably exaggerates Western decadence."[22] Did he? The examples he offered—pornography, TV stupor, intolerable music—were, as we shall see, to become far more numerous in subsequent years.

What really stuck in the craw of Solzhenitsyn's critics, however, was his Christian faith. For the *New York Times*, his was a "dangerous" worldview. At bottom, according to the *Times*, it came down to an "argument between the religious Enthusiasts, sure of their relationship to the Divine Will, and the men of the Enlightenment, trusting in the rationality of humankind." As George Will pointed out in his defense of Solzhenitsyn, the *Times*' "spacious skepticism extends to all values except its own."[23]

Newsweek solicited a critique from Olga Carlisle, a painter and journalist born in Paris of Russian descent. She and her husband had labored long years to arrange for the publication of two of Solzhenitsyn's books while he was still in the Soviet Union, but in time the author came to think that they had stalled the English translation of *The GULag Archipelago* and received excessive royalties for *The First Circle* (in its initial English translation). Feelings between Solzhenitsyn and the Carlisles reached such a pass that the couple sued him for libel; the suit was dismissed.

Newsweek's editors certainly knew all or much of this, and that is precisely why they sought Carlisle's opinion of Solzhenitsyn's address. They knew that she would seize the opportunity to settle a score. Solzhenitsyn, she said, failed to appreciate "the secular liberties formulated in the eighteenth century"; he was a spokesman "for a new, ascetic religiosity." Setting aside the personal conflict, Carlisle was like others who had initially assumed that Solzhenitsyn was, like Sakharov, a secular figure who hoped that Russia would one day adopt the ideology of the West. Disenchantment turned many of them bitter.

In 1980 the Ethics and Public Policy Center, located in Washington, DC, published *Solzhenitsyn at Harvard*, which included the address, twelve early responses, and six later critiques. Among the latter was one by Richard Pipes, a historian of Russia who taught at Harvard and who had attended Solzhenitsyn's address. He placed the famous exile in the tradition of conservative, specifically Slavophile, thought, and he was not far wrong to do so. Nineteenth-century Slavophiles, such as Alexei Khomyakov and Ivan Kireevsky, sought to defend Russia's unique traditions, to uphold the cultural centrality of the Orthodox Church, and to oppose Westernizing tendencies. As a critic of Slavophilism,

Pipes took issue with Solzhenitsyn's insistence that spiritual/moral improvement was more efficacious than political and social reform. "Apart from a handful of saintly natures," he wrote, "human beings cannot dedicate themselves to moral improvement if they are unable to satisfy their basic wants."[24] This was simply a restatement of the familiar argument for the priority of the material over the spiritual.

Pipes was himself something of a conservative (he served for a time in the Reagan administration) but of a decidedly secular sort; that is, he concerned himself almost exclusively with political and social questions, as opposed to the more profound and enduring questions of human existence. Moreover, he was a noted Russophobe who disliked Solzhenitsyn for personal reasons. As he reported in his memoirs, in 1975 he had sent the Russian a copy of one of his books, *Russia under the Old Regime*—along with a letter and personal dedication. A year later, in the course of an address at the Hoover Institution, Solzhenitsyn "delivered a blistering attack on me and my book" because it linked tsarism with communism. From that moment on, Pipes regarded him as a "fanatic" and a "false prophet."[25]

Like Pipes, Sidney Hook was an anticommunist who nevertheless insisted upon a secular view of life and the world. He admired Solzhenitsyn's courage and opposition to communism but not his "criticism of secular rational humanism." He was confident that all those opposed to totalitarianism could "work out a unifying moral program that is independent of all our theological and religious differences."[26] Unfortunately, he did not explain of what the foundation for a nonreligious morality might consist.

Ronald Berman, a former chairman of the National Endowment for the Humanities, placed Solzhenitsyn squarely in the conservative tradition of counter-Enlightenment thought—and with good reason. The Russian did sometimes sound rather like Edmund Burke or T. S. Eliot, but Berman went too far when he asserted that Russian Orthodox beliefs did "not supply the essence of his argument."[27] According to Joseph Pearce, a Catholic writer whom Solzhenitsyn received at his home in Russia in the late 1990s and to whom he granted long interviews, it was during the late seventies and early eighties that his "Russian Orthodox faith was becoming an increasingly important part of his life. Everyone in the house in Vermont wore a cross, [Great] Lent was observed rigorously and Easter [Pascha] was more important than Christmas. The children's saints' days were celebrated as enthusiastically as their birthdays and there was an Orthodox chapel in the library annex where services were said whenever a priest came to the house."[28]

The deepening of Solzhenitsyn's Russian Orthodox faith of which Pearce wrote had much to do with the friendship he sought and established with Father Alexander Schmemann, dean of St. Vladimir's Orthodox Theological Seminary. Born in Tallinn, Estonia, in 1921 to a Russian family (of Baltic German descent), Fr. Alexander moved to Paris in early childhood. His parents enrolled him and his twin brother in the Corps of Cadets, a Russian military school near Versailles. From there he enrolled in the Lycée Carnot in Paris. After completing four years, he continued his studies at a Russian *gymnasium* and in 1940 began a five-year program of study at St. Sergius Orthodox Theological Institute. Despite the war, he married in 1943 and completed his program in 1945. Ordained a priest in the same year, he soon began to teach at the institute.

Fr. Alexander was a man of culture as well as of faith. In particular he loved the literature of Russia and France. Although he and his wife were at home in France, they were parents of three children and had to live on a small income. When, therefore, Fr. Alexander received a call from St. Vladimir's, then in New York City, he accepted with alacrity and in 1951 sailed to the United States—and a new life. Founded in 1938, St. Vladimir's came into its own when Fr. Georges Florovsky arrived from St. Sergius to become dean.

From the standpoint of his future relationship with Solzhenitsyn—and of his financial viability—it was of the greatest importance that Fr. Alexander began in 1952 to make twice-weekly broadcasts to the Soviet Union over Radio Liberty. In the beginning he gave sermons, but in time he turned to literary topics and to discussions of other religions, such as Islam and Judaism; altogether he delivered over three thousand radio addresses.

Solzhenitsyn listened attentively to Fr. Alexander's broadcasts and had for them the greatest respect, as is shown in a personal letter he wrote, probably to Nikita Struve, in 1972.

> For some time now on Sunday nights, when I could, I've been listening to the Radio Liberty sermons delivered by "doctor of philosophy, Father Alexander" (his last name has never once been mentioned), and it amazes me how authentic, contemporary and eloquent the art of his preaching is. Not a note of affectation, not a millimeter of stretching the interpretation, none of the empty concessions

to required format and ritual which make a listener feel awkward or even a bit embarrassed for the preacher or for himself—but always, powerfully profound thought and profound feeling.[29]

It is not possible to say with any certainty which of Fr. Alexander's broadcasts Solzhenitsyn may have heard, but the series on the Nicene Creed would have possessed particular meaning for him. Consider the priest's wisdom concerning the horror of a fallen world—"that evil not only has dominion, but poses as something good, always hiding behind the mask of good. Evil guarantees its domination of the world by parading itself as good! Now in our own day as well, it is always in the name of good, of freedom, of concern for mankind that people are enslaved and murdered, deceived, lied to, slandered, and destroyed. Every evil screams only one message: 'I am good!' And not only does it scream, but it demands that the people cry out tirelessly in response: 'You are good, you are freedom, you are happiness!'"[30]

For his part, Fr. Alexander came to admire Solzhenitsyn for his courage and for works such as *One Day in the Life of Ivan Denisovich* and the "Lenten Letter" to Patriarch Pimen. A close friend of Nikita Struve, Fr. Alexander published an article on Solzhenitsyn in the Struve-edited *Vestnik* in 1970. In it he praised his subject for being a *Russian* rather than a *Soviet* writer, but even more important a *Christian* writer. He did not then know whether or not Solzhenitsyn was a believer; by "Christian writer" he meant that his *perception* of the world was born and grew from Biblical and Christian revelation.

That perception was the "*triune intuition of creation, fall, and redemption.*" By the intuition of creation, Fr. Alexander meant a recognition and acceptance of the original goodness of the world and life. The intuition of the fall was an understanding of evil that did not look to "systems" or "structures" but to men and the choices they make. In Solzhenitsyn's work, evil is man's betrayal of his humanity; it is his *fall*. The intuition of redemption "is an indestructible faith in the possibility of *regeneration* for man" if only he found "his conscience."[31] In 1972 Solzhenitsyn sent a letter to *Vestnik* in which he thanked Fr. Alexander for explaining "me to myself" and formulating "important traits of Christianity which I could not have formulated myself."[32]

Within days after being expelled from the Soviet Union, Solzhenitsyn told Nikita Struve that he wanted to meet Fr. Alexander. In a letter addressed to the priest and dated March 30, 1974, he extended a personal invitation. "Nikita told me that you were planning a trip to Europe. Why not come for a few days, there is so much to talk about. I am facing a problem that I cannot really understand—the number of Orthodox Churches abroad. But more important, I want to say Confession to you and take Communion. So does my whole family. Is it possible?"[33]

Indeed it was. From May 28–31, Fr. Alexander visited the Solzhenitsyns in Zurich. In his journals he wrote of driving up to the mountain cottage, which was spartan. On a long walk Solzhenitsyn asked many questions and spoke of his first marriage, his work-in-progress on the Revolution, of life, soul, and faith. "The West," Fr. Alexander discovered to his dismay, "does not exist for him." When he said "here," he meant Russia! Later that year, at New Year's Eve in Paris (which for Solzhenitsyn "was that of the Russian emigration"[34]), the Schmemanns dined with the Solzhenitsyns and the Struves—at a Russian restaurant. At the stroke of midnight *in Russia*, Solzhenitsyn jumped up and left the restaurant![35] This was in keeping with his lack of sympathy for Western political norms. "Absolute denial of democracy. Yes to monarchy."[36]

By early 1975, then, Fr. Alexander, his admiration for Solzhenitsyn still formidable, had come to recognize that there existed unbridgeable differences between them. "For him there is only Russia. For me, Russia could disappear, die, and nothing would change in my fundamental vision of the world."[37] As time went by, this difference disappointed Fr. Alexander more and more, without, however, weakening his affection and admiration for his friend.[38] Nor did Solzhenitsyn ever waver in *his* affection and admiration for his spiritual guide.

That Solzhenitsyn sometimes seemed to confuse Russia with Orthodoxy is true, though perhaps it would be closer to the truth to say that in his eyes the two were inextricably intertwined. It is also well to remember that, until his forced exile, he never knew life outside of Russia—wartime was not normal living. Fr. Alexander, on the other hand, never lived in Russia; for him, France and then America was home. Russia's true calling, in his view, "was to overcome the terrible gulf between East and West,"[39] to ascend from the lower—ethnic—unity to the higher unity in God.[40]

And yet, in a journal entry dated February 11, 1974, at the time of Solzhenitsyn's expulsion, Fr. Alexander wrote that if the exiled writer "were to ask my advice, what to do in exile, I would tell him that the Russia which expelled you is not Russia, but the Russia 'abroad' is not Russia either. Remain what you are. Be responsible; do not identify yourself with anyone or anything in the West."[41]

In any event, Fr. Alexander's disappointment with what he called Solzhenitsyn's "idolizing obsession with Russia" always seemed to leave him when the two friends were in direct contact. On May 1, 1975, this journal entry: "Yesterday morning, a phone call from Solzhenitsyn. As usual, hearing his voice I become reconciled with him; all doubts, disagreements, perplexities disappear."[42]

A week later, Fr. Alexander spends a few days with Solzhenitsyn in Canada and finds more defects of character. He lacks any sense of life's complexity and any understanding of people. He mistrusts others, is very secretive, and excessively self-assured. In some ways, he is childlike. And yet, none of these defects contradicts his greatness and literary genius. "A great man! In the obsession with his vocation, his mission, in the total identification with it—without a doubt, a great man."[43]

Fr. Alexander never lost his belief that Solzhenitsyn was a great, if driven, man, but nor could he escape the feeling that on some matters he would never see eye to eye with his admired friend. He never mistook Russia for the Church, as he believed Solzhenitsyn did. Perhaps even more important, he rejected Solzhenitsyn's hostile attitude toward the West. Near the end of his life, he confided to his journal that "I feel every year more and more strongly my own Westernism—not metaphysically, not dogmatically, but in the West I feel at home." Still, during Holy Week in 1980, Fr. Alexander and Matushka Juliana spent two days in Vermont with the Solzhenitsyns. "Our best time together. Any tension has disappeared, any caution, armor. Simple, friendly, family-like."[44] It was, taken all in all, a moving friendship.

died?

Fr. Alexander Schmemann reposed, a victim of brain cancer, on December 13, 1983. Earlier that year Solzhenitsyn had traveled to London to receive the Templeton Prize for Progress in Religion. He began the lecture he delivered on that occasion[45] by expressing his dismay that the entire twentieth century had been "sucked into the vortex of atheism and self-destruction."

How did that happen in Russia? In earlier centuries, "the Orthodox faith in our country became part of the very patterns of thought and the personality of our people, the forms of daily life, the work calendar, the priorities in every undertaking, the organization of the week and of the year." In the seventeenth century, however, Russian Orthodoxy was weakened by an internal schism— the Old Believers' refusal to accept Patriarch Nikon's reforms. In the following century, as a result of Peter the Great's program of Westernization, Russia began a process of secularization that continued to advance in the nineteenth century; by the time of the Revolution, the educated classes had lost all religious belief.

It was Dostoevsky, Solzhenitsyn told his audience, who recognized that "revolution must necessarily begin with atheism." That was unmistakably true of Russia's Revolution. For Marxists, "hatred of God is the principal driving force, more fundamental than all their political and economic pretensions. Militant atheism is not merely incidental or marginal to Communist policy; it is not a side effect, but the central pivot." That truth was demonstrated by the example of Khrushchev, who undertook some real steps in the direction of greater freedom while at the same time he "rekindled the frenzied Leninist obsession with destroying religion."

The West, Solzhenitsyn said, had yet to experience such a fanatical assault on Christianity, but the hatred that atheist zealots directed toward the faith had already had an effect; growing numbers of men had forgotten God. Without asking that Protestant, Roman Catholic, or Orthodox Christians merge or revise their doctrines, Solzhenitsyn concluded with a call for "a common front against atheism" accompanied by a renewed spirit of repentance.

When in England, Solzhenitsyn granted an interview, conducted by Michael Charlton, to the BBC. In the course of the discussion, he identified one of the primary tasks of an artist: "To fight for our memory, for our memory of what things were like. . . . A people which no longer remembers has lost its history and its soul. Yes, the main thing is to re-create. When I sit down to write, my only task is to re-create everything as it happened."[46]

It was to reclaim memory, to recover truth about the past, that Solzhenitsyn devoted so many years and so much effort, often under the most harrowing of circumstances, to *The Red Wheel*, the novelized history of the Russian Revolution that he considered the most important work of his life. First conceived in 1937, when he was still a Marxist, and distinguished by the inclusion of historical documents, newspaper excerpts, cinematic scripts, biographies, and long sections of unadulterated history, *The Red Wheel* runs to some six thousand pages. The author gained initial inspiration for the more unorthodox features of his work from John Dos Passos, whose novel *1919* (volume 2 of the U.S.A. trilogy) he had, he told Nikita Struve, read in the Lubyanka.

Still, the profoundly historical character of *The Red Wheel* is primarily a result of Solzhenitsyn's resolve to break through the distortions and outright lies told about Russia's history from 1914 to 1922 and to revivify historical memory. His title refers to the gathering and ultimately unstoppable forces of revolution—a giant wheel that turns with ever greater momentum until it is out of control. Solzhenitsyn did not mean by this that historical events were determined by impersonal forces, that free will was an illusion—that was the position taken by Marxists and Tolstoyans. In his view, nothing is inevitable; history is radically contingent. The Revolution resulted from the action (or inaction) of men and women who could have chosen different paths.

As Solzhenitsyn knew, the decision with respect to determinacy or contingency is among the most important that a historian must make; everything depends upon it. Many historians render their decision implicitly, but like Solzhenitsyn, Henry Ashby Turner, Jr., the author of *Hitler's Thirty Days to Power: January 1933*, made his explicitly. In his detailed study of those crucial days, Turner showed that there was nothing inevitable about Hitler's rise to power, that his success was the result of the actions taken by Franz von Papen, Kurt von Schleicher, Oskar von Hindenburg, Otto Meissner, Alfred Hugenberg, and others; "for although impersonal forces may make events possible, people make events happen."[47]

Those whom Turner identified bore the principal responsibility not only for President Paul von Hindenburg's decision to appoint Hitler chancellor of Germany on January 30, 1933, but for much else. "If one traces many chains of causation that have shaken the world since January 1933 back to their origins, it becomes apparent that a great deal of what has happened since then was contingent on the turn taken by German politics during that month." Had General von Schleicher or some other military officer established a government by presidential emergency decree, Europe and the world would have been spared World War II, the Holocaust, and the Cold War. Turner concluded, in words that Solzhenitsyn could have written, that the story of how Hitler achieved power "serves as a reminder that nothing except change itself is inevitable in human affairs, that the acts of individuals make a difference, and that heavy moral responsibility weighs upon those who wield control over the state."[48]

Despite its imposing length, *The Red Wheel* was to have been even longer, but not even Solzhenitsyn could complete his projected reconstruction of the years beginning with the Great War and ending with the Red victory in Russia's civil war. That is why he subtitled *The Red Wheel* "A Narrative in Discrete Periods of Time." Each period of time was a "knot"—a detailed narrative of a brief but pivotal moment on the road to revolution: Knot I (August 1914); Knot II (November 1916 [October in the Russian original because Russia was then on the Julian calendar, 13 days behind the Gregorian]); Knot III (March 1917); and Knot IV (April 1917).

Solzhenitsyn dated Knot I August 1914 (August 23–September 3) because the Great War impelled Russia toward revolution. In fact, it is not too much to say that without the war the Bolsheviks would never have come to power. We know that Russia entered the fray woefully unprepared; she lacked modern communication systems (her wireless messages were uncoded), and her supply and transport system was hopelessly out of date. Worse, her general staff had foolishly promised to launch an offensive into East Prussia no later than the fifteenth day of mobilization, a promise that the French called due as German forces neared the Marne. Considering herself duty bound, Russia sent two armies into East Prussia while, at the same time, she ordered five armies into Galicia in the main assault against Austria-Hungary. This, as Solzhenitsyn pointed out, was folly of the most irresponsible kind.

We recall that Solzhenitsyn had been an officer in the Soviet army that invaded East Prussia near the end of World War II, and his account of war in that region of Europe owed much to his own experience of combat. It did not, however, take a war veteran to recognize that catastrophe loomed; it struck near Tannenberg, where Russia's Second Army, under the command of General Aleksandr Samsonov, was almost completely destroyed. From this devastating defeat, the Russian army was never to recover. "Our morale," Solzhenitsyn wrote, "was crushed from the first and we never regained our old self-assurance."[49]

Solzhenitsyn displayed much sympathy for General Samsonov, treating him as a tragic representative of a dying regime. The general's suicide served as a premonition of the approaching death of an old regime unable, or unwilling, either to reform itself or to end the battlefield slaughter.

No one recognizes the tsar's weakness and his government's incompetence more than the fictional Colonel Georgi Vorotyntsev, who speaks for Solzhenitsyn. For the colonel, as for Solzhenitsyn, Russia was always "the true cause."[50] But the Vorotyntsev/Solzhenitsyn identity is more than a matter of common convictions. The colonel is trapped in a joyless marriage to Alina, who like Natalya Reshetovskaya is an outstanding pianist. Like Solzhenitsyn, he recognizes that he bears some responsibility for the marriage's failure. "She had every right to reprove him for his coldness, his lack of consideration for others, his fits of gloom, his absorption in himself—she rebuked him regularly and he could not blame her." And yet "every scolding left a bitter taste in his mouth."[51] Alina, like Natalya, loved social occasions, while he and Solzhenitsyn preferred a quiet existence.

In the novel, Vorotyntsev begins an affair with Olda Andozerskaya, who reminds one of Alya, Solzhenitsyn's second wife. She is a professor of medieval history not only because she believes in the subject's importance but also because it is safer in an academic environment dominated by the left. Alya chose to study mathematics because it was less policed by Soviet censors than were the humanities. Both women are intelligent and courageous opponents of the left.

Early on, Colonel Vorotyntsev recognizes that the war can only lead Russia to disaster, and he does everything in his power to promote the cause of peace on any honorable terms. He knows full well that the revolutionaries and their sympathizers among the "educated public" view the war as little more than an opportunity to advance their long-sought goal of overthrowing tsarist rule. For them revolution is literally a sacred cause, terror a religion. "Terror, and only terror," one of the "educated" declares, "leads revolution by the hand! ... You must look not at terror itself but at its lofty aims. Terrorists do not kill this or that individual—in his person they are endeavoring to kill evil itself!"[52]

Solzhenitsyn reminded those who had forgotten, or those who never knew, of the self-appointed killers of evil. What is perhaps most singular is that so many agents of terror were women. In 1878, Vera Zasulich shot and seriously wounded Fyodor Trepov, the governor of St. Petersburg. Her trial, Solzhenitsyn wrote, "was a still more glorious moment in Russian revolutionary history than her pistol shot." Her lawyer argued that it was Trepov who should be in the dock (for his brutal treatment of prisoners), and the jury returned a verdict of not guilty—"not guilty of anything at all. A bright moment in Russian history."[53]

Born to an aristocratic family, Sofia Perovskaya served on the executive committee of *Narodnaya Volya* (the People's Will), the terrorist group that organized the assassination of Tsar Aleksandr II. She was, Solzhenitsyn reported, an admirer of Rakhmetov (in Chernyshevsky's *What Is to Be Done?*) and a woman possessed of an iron will. Vera Figner, another member of *Narodnaya Volya*, attempted to resurrect the organization after the arrests following the tsar's assassination. Dora Brilliant's "big black eyes shone with the holy joy of terrorism." She was a member of the Terrorist Brigade of the Social Revolutionary Party and an expert maker of bombs. Maria Spiridonova assassinated a police official in 1905, thereby guaranteeing herself a place of honor among heroines of the terrorist faith. "Profound belief in a sacred cause," Solzhenitsyn wrote, "that is what inspired them all."[54]

Not all terrorists, of course, were women. Solzhenitsyn recalled the extraordinary career of Ivan Kalyaev, a man who inspired—if that is the word—Albert Camus and the young György Lukács.[55] Known to his comrades as "the poet," Kalyaev joined the so-called Terrorist Brigade in 1903. Of this intense young man, Boris Savinkov, himself a noted terrorist, observed that "his love of art and the revolution was illumined by the same fire that animated his soul—his furtive, unconscious but strong and deep religious instinct."[56] This instinct meant that everything was *not* permitted. He refused, for example, to throw a bomb into Grand Duke Sergei's carriage because the duchess and two children were with him. Two days later, however, he found the Grand Duke alone and murdered him.

What appealed to Camus and Lukács was the fact that Kalyaev, unlike most terrorists, never claimed that the end justified the means. The end—the destruction of the tsarist system—was a noble one in his eyes, but the means employed—murder—could never be justified morally. He was willing to pay for his crime with his life, in that way affirming both his action *and* his responsibility. More than his life, he was prepared to sacrifice his moral purity for his fellowmen.

Solzhenitsyn recognized in Kalyaev and other terrorists, but also in their admirers among the "educated public," a religious instinct that was perverted and misdirected. It was perverted because by linking religion with atheism, it provided the latter with a spiritual aura that could make a criminal act appear to be a sacrament. It was misdirected for the reason that Solzhenitsyn suggested in a conversation between his fictional characters. "You speak of ordering and perfecting society," one of them says. "But nothing is more precious to a man than the order in his own soul, not even the welfare of remote generations."[57] That did not mean that nothing should be done to reform a government or a social order; Solzhenitsyn emphasized throughout *The Red Wheel* that reform of the old regime was an absolute necessity. It meant that man's primary duty was the perfecting of his own soul.

It is difficult to know with any certainty what Dimitri Bogrov hoped to perfect when, on September 1, 1911, he carried out what one fictional admirer in *The Red Wheel* called "the crowning achievement of Russian terrorism!"

That "achievement" was the assassination of Pyotr Stolypin, prime minister of Russia and an authoritarian reformer possessed of many personal and political gifts. Stolypin was, Solzhenitsyn believed, the one and only great man in the years leading up to war and revolution, a man who, had he lived, might have spared Russia the agonies of both. Nevertheless, after his death his enemies in the old and Soviet regimes had "disfigured his memory with lie upon lie."[58]

So determined was Solzhenitsyn to bring truth and honor to Stolypin's memory that, in the pages devoted to him, he added nothing fictional. The prime minister was hated by the left—and not merely the revolutionaries—primarily because of his refusal to treat terrorists with leniency and "understanding." "Stolypin told himself that the tougher he was to begin with, the fewer lives would be lost in the end. Excessive leniency at the beginning could only increase the number of victims later. He would use conciliatory methods where persuasion was possible. But the mad dogs would not be converted by persuasion—swift and relentless punishment was the only thing for them."[59]

Above all, Solzhenitsyn admired Stolypin for his love of *Russia*. "You," the prime minister told a defiant Duma, "are after great upheavals, we are after a great Russia."[60] To that end he outlined a reform plan to turn the peasants' allotment of land in the commune—viewed by the left as a ready-made socialist institution—into permanent (private) property. Transforming peasants into smallholders was the key to their prosperity and allegiance to the tsarist government. Solzhenitsyn cited Stolypin's words to members of the Duma, most of whom turned a deaf ear: "The government wishes to see the peasant rich and self-sufficient, and with prosperity come enlightenment and real freedom. To this end the able and hardworking Russian peasant, salt of the earth, must be given the opportunity to free himself from his present trammels. We must deliver him from slavery to the obsolete commune, give him control over his land."[61]

In accord with a decree of November 9, 1907, the Russian peasant obtained the right to leave the commune, consolidate his allotment as a private holding, or, if he pleased, separate himself completely from the village and set up a farm with its own house. And that was only the beginning of Stolypin's sweeping reform program. The prime minister "considered local self-government scarcely less of a blessing for Russia than the reorganization of peasant farming in smallholdings. In his first months in power he began energetically reviving the zemstvos."[62] These provincial assemblies (abolished by the Bolsheviks) were one of the results of the Great Reforms of the 1860s, largely the work of Nikolai Miliutin, a conservative liberal of outstanding ability, and approved by Tsar Aleksandr II. They provided a degree of local self-government to all elements of the population.

Stolypin, a profoundly religious man, proclaimed what Solzhenitsyn himself believed: "The Russian state and the Christian Church are bound together by ties many centuries old."[63] At the same time, the prime minister guaranteed the Old Believers equal rights with the Orthodox and drafted a law granting equal rights to the Jews—the latter rejected by Nicholas II. A farsighted reformer, Stolypin rejected any notion that Russia copy Western institutions; she had to follow her own path. It is no wonder that Solzhenitsyn revered him.

During Stolypin's years as prime minister (1906–1911), however, few members of Russia's ruling class and virtually no one among the intelligentsia felt a similar reverence. The tsar was always notably cool toward him, and too many on the right refused to support his reforms, preferring a "petrified immobility, century after century."[64] For those on the left, of course, he was the devil himself. They were pleased to celebrate his murder—and his murderer.

Like so many assassins, Dmitri Bogrov was a loner, a man who lived in the shadows. Born to a family of wealthy Jewish merchants, he studied law and persuaded himself that the best way to bring down the government was to kill its most important officials. An anarcho-communist, he eschewed political parties; in fact, he reported on leftist parties to the Okhrana (political police). Was he then another Yevno Azef, a double agent who worked for the Okhrana but masterminded the assassinations of Minister of the Interior V. K. von Plehve (1904) and Grand Duke Sergei (1905)? That question haunted many admirers of Bogrov's deed. For them, "Azef" stood for "some sort of terrible, loathsome treachery than which there was nothing worse."[65]

Solzhenitsyn did not take Bogrov to be another Azef. Stolypin's assassin, he insisted, provided the Okhrana with information it already possessed. In this, he was mistaken. Due to the information Bogrov passed on to the police "several expropriations, attacks by revolutionaries on banks and other institutions to steal money, were prevented and a number of revolutionaries were arrested."[66] Perhaps he hoped to atone for those sins by taking Stolypin's life—we simply do not know what prompted him to act. We do know that the opportunity for which he had been looking presented itself on September 1, 1911 (O.S.) when Stolypin (as well as the tsar and his children) attended a gala performance of Nikolai Rimsky-Korsakov's opera *The Tale of Tsar Saltan* at

Kiev's City Theater. The occasion was the fiftieth anniversary of Tsar Aleksandr II's liberation of the serfs.

Told by Bogrov that Stolypin might be the target of an assassination attempt, Lieutenant Colonel N. N. Kulyabko gave his agent a ticket to the opera; the assassin entered the theater unchallenged and carrying a Browning revolver. During the second intermission he walked to the orchestra section where the prime minister was standing and in conversation. He fired two shots—one to the victim's right hand and one to his chest. The second bullet proved to be fatal; Stolypin died four days later. Bogrov was tried and convicted by a military court and hanged on September 11.

As Solzhenitsyn pointed out, it pleased liberal society to regard Bogrov as an Okhrana agent and hence a rightist. And for reasons of his own, Nicholas II pardoned all those—and they were numerous—who shared responsibility for the assassination. This was the final insult as far as Solzhenitsyn was concerned. But even more important: "How simple it had proved in the end to change the course of history: all you had to do was get a theater ticket, walk past seventeen rows of seats, and press a trigger."[67] Not the logic of economic development or some inescapable destiny, but the conscious action of one man signaled the death of a dynasty.

Memories of Stolypin, and of what might have been, color all of Knot II, November 1916 (October 27–November 17). Frustrated by the weakness of the tsar and the incompetence of his ministers, Colonel Vorotyntsev can scarcely contain himself. They had rejected the martyred prime minister and "given him to the assassin. (If everything was still in Stolypin's firm hands, either this war would never have happened or it would have been fought differently)."[68] The members of educated society were no better; they had done nothing but abuse and revile him.

For the party of Russian liberalism, the Constitutional Democratic Party (popularly the "Kadets"), Vorotyntsev (Solzhenitsyn) reserves a particular animus. Founded in 1905 and led by the historian Pavel Milyukov, the party was decidedly of the left. "Its program," Solzhenitsyn observed, "showed the leftward dislocation of the neck obligatory for radicals the world over." Fearing to be associated with the right, the Kadets had opposed Stolypin at every turn and wanted nothing more than to witness the collapse of the autocracy. Solzhenitsyn portrayed Milyukov as reckless, ambitious, and self-admiring, a scholar whose work was discredited by its "inaccuracy in the use of sources, intrusive 'conclusions' instead of factual history, jealous concern for his own reputation."[69]

To whom, then, could Vorotyntsev turn? He certainly felt an affinity for D. N. Shipov, a liberal of the right and a prominent zemstvo activist. "The Kadets," Shipov observed, "were indifferent, if not hostile, to religion. Their own irreligion made it difficult for them to understand the real spirit of the people. This was why, while sincerely striving to better the lives of the masses, they tended to corrupt the soul of the people by encouraging manifestations of spite and hatred."[70]

Solzhenitsyn summarized Shipov's philosophy of life and social program in sympathetic terms. While the zemstvo leader recognized that the inner development of the person was more important than social development, he insisted that "no Christian has the right to be indifferent to the social order." It was wrong in his (and Solzhenitsyn's) judgment to believe that all power was of divine origin and that it had therefore to be accepted in its existing form. A monarchist critical of parliamentary systems, he nevertheless believed that people, as they gained political experience, had a legitimate role to play in public life. The best way to obtain that experience was through "participation in local—zemstvo or municipal—self-government."[71]

Shipov was a good and thoughtful man but, as Solzhenitsyn pointed out, one incapable of action. This was less true of Shipov's colleague Aleksandr Guchkov, a military adventurer and wealthy industrialist who in 1905 helped to found the conservative Union of 17 October (date of the tsar's October Manifesto that granted basic civil liberties and limited power to a state duma, or parliament). Guchkov, who was prominent in the Third Duma (elected 1907), favored a reform-minded constitutional monarchy and "recognized in Stolypin a man of action, strong-willed and clear-minded, with a definite view on every question, straightforward in all his pronouncements—and one in whom 'things Russian are at the center of everything.'"[72] Of Nicholas II he thought a good deal less, especially after assuming the office of Duma president in 1910.

It was not long before the tsar formed an unfavorable opinion of Guchkov, who among other sins spoke out publicly against Rasputin. Nor could he or his middle-of-the-road policies expect any sympathy or support from the political left or right. His fortunes continued to decline until, on the eve of war, the right and center of his own party, the Octobrist, broke with him. "Still at the height of his powers," Solzhenitsyn wrote, "he was denied any chance of using them; renowned throughout Russia, he was suddenly of no use to anyone."[73]

When war broke out, Guchkov, always lured by adventure, headed for the front, where he served with the Red Cross. Early on he recognized the hopelessness of Russia's effort, and by the fall of 1916, he had begun to fasten his meager hopes upon a palace revolution that might save Russia and the monarchy. In one of the most dramatic fictional sections *of November 1916*, Vorotyntsev meets Guchkov, whose martial and civic courage he admired. He had hopes of finding some way to help end the war.

Vorotyntsev is greatly pleased when Guchkov proposes to do something to forestall a revolution. "It's no good sitting around waiting like drooling idiots for a dainty little revolution," Guchkov says. "We must use our minds and our will to stop revolution!" And then, finally: "The Emperor, who cannot be parted from his witch of a wife, must be made to give up the throne. A palace revolution is Russia's only salvation."[74] Guchkov calculates that he would need one or two military units to carry out the planned coup and places his hopes on Vorotyntsev.

The colonel might well have been willing to act had Guchkov not let slip that the coup would ensure future victories in the war. In that sense he was no different from the tsar and the Kadets—all of them were devoted to the Allies and to the continuation of the struggle. Vorotyntsev "had found no cause worthy of his efforts. And now there was this other problem: what did the future hold for Alina and himself?"[75] Having to confront this problem and having found no resolute opponents of the war, he himself was paralyzed.

Troubled by guilt, but deeply in love with Olda, Vorotyntsev decides to tell Alina of his affair. She is not, he learns quickly, all forgiving—in fact, she threatens suicide. He is at a loss to know where to turn, but he knows that he will not give up Olda. The space that Solzhenitsyn devotes to this love triangle obviously reflects his own inner struggles as his first marriage was collapsing and he was already involved with Alya. But it is also a way of suggesting the paralysis of those who wished to place a spoke in the wheel of revolution.

Back briefly at GHQ in Mogilev, Vorotyntsev encounters General Aleksandr Nechvolodov (an actual historical figure). The senior officer's thoughts, like those of the colonel, are of Russia alone. He knows that the press, the teachers, and the educated public are hoping for revolution, but he also knows that too many on the right hounded Stolypin, "a man capable of dragging Russia out of the slough by sheer force."[76] An authentic and intelligent right scarcely existed, and thus there was no one ready to lead, no one prepared to act; revolution was at the door.

No thanks to Lenin, who remained safely in exile while others did the Bolsheviks' work in Russia. The leading figure there was Aleksandr Shlyapnikov, held in contempt by Lenin, but for whom, as we have seen, Solzhenitsyn retained a good bit of respect. Not the least of his reasons was that Shlyapnikov was born to a family of Old Believers. He had, Solzhenitsyn maintained, been ready to die for his people, but when, thanks to Stolypin, their persecutions ended, the energies of their young flowed into other channels. "Aleksandr was converted to Social Democracy. A completely different cause, on the face of it, but the enemy, the persecutors, were the same as before."[77]

But there was also the fact that Shlyapnikov was a worker who never lost his concern for living, breathing workers (rather than what Martin Malia called a "metaphysical proletariat"[78]). He began factory work at the age of thirteen and for many years labored in factories in western Europe—for him a true International. He never tired of working with his hands. "Your happiest days," Solzhenitsyn wrote of him rather idealistically, "are still those spent not on committees, at strike meetings, in demonstrations, or with émigré politicians, no, it's when you walk into some place that's all cheerful noise and cogs and pinions and crankshafts and helical gears, and you know every move you need to make, and do it your own way, and hear simple words of praise from the old hands, then from the foreman—that's where you really feel at home!"[79]

While in western Europe, Shlyapnikov met Alexandra Kollontai, a revolutionary and advocate of "free love" who was twelve years his senior. Well educated, she became his mentor. Lenin had little use for either of them, but after the Bolsheviks seized power, he appointed Shlyapnikov commissar of labor and Kollontai commissar for public welfare. Alienated by the Party's dictatorial control of the trade unions, Shlyapnikov and Kollontai formed the Workers' Opposition, which proved to be short-lived. At the Tenth Party Congress in 1921, Lenin declared that "this is no time for an opposition."[80] Kollontai managed to survive as a diplomat, but Shlyapnikov remained under suspicion. Once Stalin had consolidated his power, he ordered the latter's expulsion from the Party, imprisonment, and execution.

After parting with General Nechvolodov, Vorotyntsev sets out on a walk, the better to think more clearly about Alina, Olda, and his adultery. Along the way he happens upon a monastery and stops. "Should he go in, or shouldn't he?" He does not because he is in a rush to send a telegram to Alina, who is still threatening to take her own life.[81] The scene tells us about Solzhenitsyn when his own marriage was in turmoil and he may not yet have repented of his sins; *November 1916* concludes, however, with a tale of sexual sin and repentance.

Early in the novel, Vorotyntsev finds himself in a train compartment with Fyodor Kovynev, a forty-year-old Cossack writer and former high-school teacher. Because they are strangers and unlikely to meet again, Kovynev tells the colonel the story of his life. He has, he says, notebooks on the basis of which he plans to write a novel entitled *The Quiet Don*. This was Solzhenitsyn's way of letting his readers know that he modeled Kovynev on Fyodor Kryukov, the Cossack writer whose unpublished manuscripts had, he always insisted, been plagiarized by Mikhail Sholokhov.

But Kovynev does not restrict himself to his career plans; he shares with Vorotyntsev the details of an affair with Zinaida Altanskaya, a former student more than twenty years his junior. Initially it was she who sought to seduce him, but fearing an involvement from which he might not easily extricate himself, he leaves Tambov and takes up residence in St. Petersburg. Feeling jilted, Zinaida begins an affair with a married factory engineer and conceives a child. She insists that her lover confess to his wife, and like Vorotyntsev later in the novel, he does so. The wife, however, refuses to set her weak husband free, and Zinaida finds herself alone with an illegitimate infant.

As it often does, one sin leads to another, and Zinaida, not wishing her mother to know of her plight, does not go to her on her deathbed. With no one else to whom she can turn—she does not believe in "God the Comforter"[82]—she implores Kovynev to come to her; he is the man whom she truly wants. After some hesitation he agrees, and they begin an affair that he has no intention of prolonging and which leads to a great tragedy; while she is in Tambov with Kovynev, her son dies in the small village to which she had retreated.

Zinaida is devastated, and in search of solace, she goes to a women's monastery to visit her aunt, a nun. Though she still believes "God the Comforter" to be an absurdity, her relative helps her to begin "to recover her balance." But only to begin. Still suffering, she returns to the church in nearby Utkino where Father Aloni, who conducted a service for her son, is priest. She had not consciously intended to return; "her legs had brought her unbidden."[83] The scene at the church is the most powerful in the novel—at once a story of Solzhenitsyn's personal repentance and his hope for Russia's.

Standing before an icon of Christ, Zinaida sees His compassion for all who approach Him and understands that "He could grant release from all pain. A weight was lifted from her." As she turns from the icon, she sees that Fr. Aloni is hearing confessions. Assuming that she was waiting to make hers, he nods an invitation, and she moves to the lectern on which rest the Gospel and a crucifix. At first with difficulty, but with increasing peace, she makes her confession to God—the priest "was only the necessary witness." He says not a word until she is finished, offers her absolution, and then: "The world holds no suffering worse than those caused by family problems. They leave festering sores on the heart itself." He—and Solzhenitsyn—conclude by reminding her (us) that "there is nothing higher than love."[84]

The February (March, NS) revolution of 1917 was genuine and spontaneous. Beginning in Petrograd as bread riots on February 23/March 8, International Women's Day, it quickly developed into widespread and violent street demonstrations. Banners appeared proclaiming "Down with the War!" and "Down with the Tsar!" Shlyapnikov, head of the Bolsheviks' Central Committee in Petrograd, thought it unwise to squander valuable personnel and resources on further demonstrations, but no one was listening. In five tumultuous days, tsarist rule collapsed.

For most Western historians, this was a glorious, if short-lived, event in Russian history—the fall of autocracy and the establishment of a liberal-democratic government. Solzhenitsyn did not view it that way. He regarded the revolution as a catastrophe that prepared the way, within months, for the Bolshevik coup d'état. It was not long, he recognized, before the crowds of "demonstrators" in Petrograd turned into mobs. Once a part of a crowd, Solzhenitsyn observed, an "individual was absolved of his normal responsibilities, and his strength swelled in proportion to the number in the crowd, even as they drained him of his willpower."[85]

Released from any inner or outer restraint, and thus turned into something inhuman, people in the streets begin to smash windows and loot stores. They hurl bottles and fire shots at policemen brave enough, or foolish enough, to confront them. "Sometimes the bodies of murdered policemen were dumped in garbage pits."[86]

Frenzied mobs storm prisons and unlock the cells. "The common criminals were all set free along with the political prisoners (and far outnumber them). Within hours a wave of robberies, arson attacks, and murders breaks out all over the city."[87] The more blood that is shed, the more insatiable the blood lust. A mob of armed workers and soldiers attacks a barracks and slaughters the reservists therein.

Amid the chaos two centers of power emerge in Petrograd—the Duma and the newly organized Soviet of Workers' and Soldiers' Deputies. The Soviet hesitates to assume the responsibilities of power; hence the Duma forms a "Provisional Government" headed by Prince Georgi Lvov but soon dominated by Aleksandr Kerensky.

The Provisional Government (technically it was still a "Provisional Committee") knew that it had to secure the tsar's formal abdication. To that end, it dispatched two Duma deputies, Aleksandr Guchkov and Vasily Shulgin, to Pskov, where the imperial train, on its way from Mogilev to Tsarskoe Selo (and the tsar's family), had come, temporarily Nicholas hoped, to rest. Both Guchkov and Shulgin were monarchists who hoped that an abdication in favor of Nicholas's son Alexei (with Grand Duke Mikhail acting as regent) might yet save the monarchy and lead to a victorious conclusion to the war.

Solzhenitsyn described the frustration that Guchkov and Shulgin experienced while dealing with the tsar. Nicholas had agreed to abdicate before the Duma emissaries arrived, but he expected to be able to keep his hemophiliac son with him until the boy came of age. Being told that that would be impossible, he preferred to abdicate for his son as well—in favor of his brother. But could he, by law, do so? No one knew for certain, but Guchkov and Shulgin decided that they had to have a signed letter of abdication, law or no law. Nicholas, eager to join his family in Tsarskoe Selo, obliged on March 2. "At this decisive moment We have deemed Ourselves conscience-bound to afford Our people unity and solidarity ... and in one accord with the State Duma, We have seen fit to abdicate the throne of the Russian State.... Not wishing to be parted from Our beloved son ... we pass the succession to Our brother."[88]

On March 3, the Provisional Government gave the former tsar permission to travel to Tsarskoe Selo, but on the same day the Petrograd Soviet voted to arrest the royal family. On March 9, Nicholas arrived at Tsarskoe, where he and his family were detained under house arrest. Meanwhile, Grand Duke Mikhail, unable to receive a guarantee of safety from the Provisional Government, renounced the throne. It did not save his life; the Bolsheviks murdered him as well as Nicholas and his entire family in 1918.

Solzhenitsyn described Lenin's cynical negotiations with the Germans, who allowed him and some forty other Bolsheviks to return to Russia in a sealed railroad car. Their reason for doing so was to create anarchy in Russia and thus undermine their enemy's war effort. Arriving at the Finland Station in Petrograd, the Bolshevik chieftain declared that there should be no support for the Provisional Government and that all power should be given to the Soviet. He promised peace, land, and bread. In a chapter from *April 1917*, Solzhenitsyn tells of disabled veterans who, having sacrificed so much, despise his call for peace with Germany. "See our wounds," they yell. "They cry out for victory."[89]

The Provisional Government, faithful to its democratic principles and lacking an instinct for survival, declares that "every citizen of our new, free Russia has a right to express his opinions freely."[90] But when veterans attempt to express *their* opinions, Bolsheviks attack them physically and shower them with obscenities.

Meanwhile, Vorotyntsev, still in Mogilev, prepares to speak to hundreds of officers. He recognizes that Nechvolodov was right—the revolution is already upon Russia—and still no one has raised a finger. "However few men we can muster," the colonel thinks to himself, "neither the government nor the Council [Soviet] can deprive us of our ultimate right—the right to fight again. It has been growing and swelling, and now conflict is inevitable. The fight will surely come."[91] This was Solzhenitsyn's way of telling us that Vorotyntsev will join the White, anti-Bolshevik, forces in the approaching civil war.

Although Solzhenitsyn drove himself during the 1980s to complete the twenty "knots" that would carry his narrative through the long years of civil war, he had finally to recognize that the full project was too ambitious; Knot IV, *April 1917*, was therefore the last. As it stands, the first three knots of *The Red Wheel* comprise Act I (*Revolution*) while the fourth, together with a detailed outline of the unwritten knots, comprise Act II (*Democracy*).

While Solzhenitsyn worked on *The Red Wheel*, dramatic events were unfolding in the Soviet Union. In rapid succession, Party General Secretaries Leonid Brezhnev, Yuri Andropov, and Konstantin Chernenko died. In March 1985 a relatively young (he was in his early 50s) Mikhail Gorbachev assumed power, promising *glasnost* ("openness") and *perestroika* ("restructuring")—in other words, reform. Although he made missteps, Gorbachev was serious about reforming a system the failures of which could no longer be ignored. Initially concerned to revive a stagnant economy, he quickly recognized that nothing could be achieved without political reforms.

As the enormity of the internal tasks he had set for himself became ever clearer, Gorbachev broadened his reformist plans and took some important, and symbolic, steps. He began to replace old-line Stalinists such as Minister of Foreign Affairs Andrei Gromyko, and he invited Andrei Sakharov back to Moscow from his internal exile in Gorky. He moved, too, to end the Communist Party's monopoly on power and to allow greater freedom of speech.

Gorbachev had the further good sense to recognize that the Soviet Union could not survive if it held on to its Eastern European satellites, and he made it clear to the communist leaders in the bloc nations that they could no longer rely upon the Red Army to maintain them in power; in 1989 the communist regimes fell like dominoes. Cold War tensions eased even more as Gorbachev began to withdraw Soviet troops from Afghanistan and established good working relations with US President Ronald Reagan and British Prime Minister Margaret Thatcher.

These historic actions did not escape Solzhenitsyn's notice, especially not when, in October 1989, *Novy Mir* published long extracts from *The GULag Archipelago*. Convinced that the Soviet Union was on its last legs, he committed to paper an essay, "How to Revitalize Russia," in July 1990; the Moscow-based *Komsomolskaya Pravda* and *Literaturnaya gazeta* published it in September of the same year. An English translation entitled *Rebuilding Russia* appeared in 1991.

Certain that a major regime change was in the offing, Solzhenitsyn feared that Russia might descend into an anarchy similar to that which followed the February 1917 revolution. "Amid the [contemporary] tumult of mass meetings and of multiplying splinter parties," he wrote, "we have failed to notice that we have donned the gaudy circus attire of February—of those ill-fated eight months in 1917. And the few observers who did take note of the similarity are gushing with blind elation about 'the new February Revolution.' (To make the analogy complete, the black banners of anarchy have also made their appearance.)"[92]

Rather than a revolution that attempted to change everything at once, Solzhenitsyn recommended reforms to be instituted in a cautious and piecemeal fashion—*repair*, in all aspects of modern life, was a lost art. Although there were things to be learned from the West, he insisted that Russia look primarily to its own historical experience. He hoped to see a revival of a zemstvo system and, not surprisingly, he mentioned the name of Stolypin more than once. The martyred prime minister believed that a state governed by laws required independent citizens who, in turn, required the freedom to own their own property—particularly in land. But there was so much more to be done—establish a market economy, encourage small enterprises and prohibit monopolies, prevent further damage to the environment, reform the system of education.

All of this was important, but its successful implementation would not usher in a utopia. "The strength or weakness of a society," Solzhenitsyn reminded his readers, "depends more on the level of its spiritual life than on its level of industrialization. Neither a market economy nor even general abundance constitutes the crowning achievement of human life."[93] What Russia needed above all was personal and national repentance for sins committed during Soviet rule and a healthy spirit of self-limitation.

In the second half of his essay, Solzhenitsyn discussed forms of government. He insisted that there existed no "best" form for all peoples at all times; it depended upon the historic experience of the people in question. Following Tocqueville, whom he had read with care, he believed that "the whole flow of modern history will unquestionably predispose us to choose democracy," rather than monarchy or aristocracy.[94] But like the author of *Democracy in America*, he did not welcome the inevitable with open arms.

It was one thing to view democracy as the modern fate and to appreciate some of its virtues; it was something else to elevate it into a cult or a religion. Solzhenitsyn cited the famous observation by the Austrian-American economist and political scientist Joseph Schumpeter to the effect that democracy was the surrogate faith of intellectuals deprived of religion. And once again he recalled the unhappy experience of democracy in February 1917.

Solzhenitsyn warned against universal and equal suffrage, according to Dostoevsky "the most absurd invention of the nineteenth century."[95] Nor was he in favor of election by popular vote at every level of government, but only at the local level where voters could know candidates personally. He recommended a system of rule that combined local self-government with a strong central authority to conduct national and international policy.

And one thing more. "One might consider ... the suggestion made by Pyotr Stolypin": the institution of "a two- or three-year academy for those aspiring to top government posts."[96] In other words, the training of an elite to provide counsel and to serve where needed. The idea resembled that advanced for his own country by George Kennan, the distinguished American diplomat who served many years in Russia and who admired Solzhenitsyn. Kennan had recommended the creation of a "Council of State" that would consider long-term problems and make policy suggestions. Members of the council would be persons of high distinction and independent judgment.[97]

It is clear from *Rebuilding Russia* that Solzhenitsyn preferred a democratic form of government that shied away from an extreme egalitarianism and that maintained a strong, but nontyrannical and non-ideological, authority. In the event, it was not an outlook shared by many Russians. They were not, however, prepared to turn back from the path of reform—even when Gorbachev himself appeared to waver. In August 1991 a group of hard-liners whom he himself had appointed attempted a coup that ended in rather comic fashion. With virtually no one willing to obey the so-called "State Committee for the State of Emergency in the USSR," the coup leaders fled.

The leader of the opposition to the coup was Boris Yeltsin, who had won election as president of the newly sovereign Russian republic in June. In early December Yeltsin met with officials in Ukraine and Belorussia, and together they announced the dissolution of the Soviet Union, to which Gorbachev agreed before the end of the month. The catastrophic "experiment" of seventy-four years had come to an end—not with a bang but with a whimper.

In June 1992 Yeltsin phoned Solzhenitsyn to tell him that Russia's doors were wide open for his return and that he would do everything in his power to restore the country's spiritual and material health. The month before the call, Alya had traveled to Moscow to seek a suitable home for the return. It would not be long—but not before he made a farewell trip to western Europe. On September 14, 1993, he was in Liechtenstein, a state he admired for its modest size and stability, to address the International Academy of Philosophy on the idea of progress.[98] He did not deny that the modern world had witnessed much progress, but it was largely confined to technology; of moral and spiritual progress he perceived little evidence. At least since the Enlightenment, men had ceased to see *the purpose*—the meaning—of their existence. They had lost their way spiritually.

From Liechtenstein, Solzhenitsyn traveled to Lucs-sur-Boulogne, France, where on September 25 he spoke at the dedication of a memorial to the thousands of peasants in the Vendée (in west-central France) who had perished in a revolt against the French revolutionary government of the Terror.[99] However much leftists romanticized them, Solzhenitsyn said, revolutions such as those in France and Russia, brought "out instincts of primordial barbarism, the sinister forces of envy, greed, and hatred." It was to the eternal credit of the peasants of the Vendée that they recognized that the ideology of "Progress" resulted in false hopes, and ultimately in terror.

At the same time that he spoke departing words to the West, Solzhenitsyn penned a reflection on Russia's history and the dilemmas she faced at the end of the twentieth century. Over seventy years of communist rule had produced suffering on a scarcely imaginable scale, starting with the physical destruction of millions of lives as a result of the war with Germany and the war waged against internal "enemies." In addition, there was the destruction of the environment and the propaganda bombardment that stupefied minds and depraved souls. He could only hope, he concluded, that the Orthodox Church would be able to aid in the challenging work of Russia's renewal.

CHAPTER FIVE

THE RETURN

I n May 1994, Solzhenitsyn, Alya, and their son Stepan left Cavendish, Vermont, for the long journey home. Their route took them to Anchorage by way of Boston and Salt Lake City; from there they travelled on to Magadan, the gateway to the Kolyma region. From that place of camp memories, they proceeded to Vladivostok, where on May 27 their first-born son Yermolai and some four thousand citizens greeted them. "I never doubted that communism was doomed to collapse," Solzhenitsyn told his welcomers, "but I was always fearful that our exit from it, the price of it, would be terribly painful."[1]

Yermolai accompanied his father on a two-month journey across Siberia, while Alya and Stepan flew to Moscow to make their new home ready. Father and son arrived in the capital on July 21—and despite the realism he had expressed in Vladivostok, Solzhenitsyn was shocked, and not only because of communism's legacy. "The West was moving in. Send us your trivia, your TV game shows, your dazzling trash, your pornography!"[2] He was perhaps less shocked to find that the new Russian elite considered him to be a man of the past.

As Solzhenitsyn settled into his secluded home in a wooded area outside of Moscow, he formed an unfavorable opinion of Boris Yeltsin, even though the Russian president's family was descended from Old Believers. In December 1985, after Yeltsin had served as party boss of Sverdlovsk Oblast (where he carried out orders to destroy the house in which the Bolsheviks murdered the tsar and his family), Gorbachev brought him to Moscow to serve as first secretary of the city's Communist Party. Almost immediately, Yeltsin began to complain about the slow pace of Gorbachev's reforms and to seek power for himself. In June 1991 he won election to the new post of president of the Russian Soviet Federative Socialist Republic, and following the dissolution of the USSR he continued in office as president of the Russian Federation.

Adept at conducting political campaigns, Yeltsin found governing to be more of a challenge, not least because, on the advice of economist Yegor Gaidar, he was determined to transform Russia overnight by means of "shock therapy," that is radical reforms. The unintended result was a latter-day "Time of Troubles" (the first "Time of Troubles," 1598–1613, preceded the establishment of the Romanov dynasty). The troubles included corruption, inflation rates as high as 2,600 percent, and economic disaster for millions of Russians—though not for the "oligarchs," who bought up the vouchers given to all citizens as part of a privatization program. As the 1996 presidential election approached, Solzhenitsyn made it clear that he would not vote for Yeltsin.

Despite the heavy drinking that damaged his reputation and health (he was soon to undergo quintuple heart bypass surgery), Yeltsin won reelection. His second term in office was, however, worse than the first. The financial crisis of 1998, Solzhenitsyn told an interviewer in 2007, "was the country's low point, with people in misery."[3] In that year he published *Russia in Collapse*.[4]

In the four years since he had returned home, Solzhenitsyn wrote, he had traveled across Russia and met with people from every walk of life. What he learned from the experience was that Russians had reached the point of desperation, their trust in government all but nonexistent. Solzhenitsyn's was no greater. "With no time to look around, to adjust ourselves to the changes, to prepare ourselves and our children, to preserve the remnants of our meager property, we leapt—we were thrown—not into the 'Market,' but into a 'Market Ideology.'" After the long years of communist misrule, this latest disaster threatened the very existence of the Russian people. What—to borrow from Chernyshevsky—was to be done?

Contemporary Russians, Solzhenitsyn wrote, would be wise to take their bearings from the Old Believers. "*Them* you cannot accuse of being spoiled; or corrupt; or lazy; or unable to run an industrial, agricultural or merchant business; nor of being illiterate; nor most certainly, of being indifferent to spiritual questions." Despite terrible persecutions, they retained a national consciousness, a shared historical memory. Moreover, they knew that "the spiritual life of a nation is more important than its territory and more important, even, than its level of economic prosperity."

On December 31, 1999, Boris Yeltsin resigned as president of Russia, leaving the office to his recently named prime minister, Vladimir Putin. A former KGB lieutenant colonel and director of the FSB (Federal Security Service), Putin, Yeltsin said, could "unite around himself those who will renew Great Russia in the new 21st Century." With the advantage of being acting president, Putin won the 2000 presidential election with 53 percent of the vote, though he had told Yeltsin that he disliked election campaigns. "I don't know how to run them, and I don't like them."[5]

It was not long before Putin's popularity as president exceeded his electoral margin. To a Russian public worn out by political turmoil, he brought a welcome stability—and remarkable economic growth. Recognizing the importance of tax policy, he introduced a flat income tax of 13 percent, reduced the profit tax from 35 to 24 percent, eliminated the sales tax, reduced the payroll tax from 36 to 26 percent and the value-added tax from 20 to 18 percent.[6] He turned the federal budget deficit into a surplus, reduced the burden of regulation on small businesses, and curbed the "oligarchs." On his watch the middle class grew dramatically and the number of people below the poverty line decreased greatly.

Although criticized by some of the Russian press (for which he had little use) and the entire Western press as "undemocratic," Putin operated well within the democratic framework, even if his personal style was authoritarian. Determined to maintain a proper public order, he was an enemy of tyranny and ideological indoctrination. He chose as his model Pyotr Stolypin, whom he described as "a true patriot and a wise politician who saw that all kinds of radical sentiment and procrastination, a refusal to launch the necessary reform, were dangerous to the country, and that only a strong and effective government relying on business and the civil initiative of millions could ensure progressive development."[7] Like Stolypin, too, Putin refused to temporize with terrorists, particularly Chechens; "I have never for a second believed," he said, "that Chechnya would limit itself to its own independence. It would become a beachhead for further attacks on Russia."[8]

Putin based his foreign policy on the national interest of Russia, not that of Western nations. After initial efforts to establish a cooperative relationship with the United States, for example, he grew weary of being lectured to about "democracy and human rights." His defense of Russian interests, respect for Stolypin, and competent leadership earned Solzhenitsyn's praise. "Putin," Solzhenitsyn told Der Spiegel, "inherited a ransacked and bewildered country, with a poor and demoralized people. And he started to do what was possible—a slow and gradual restoration."[9]

Solzhenitsyn also admired Putin's profession of Russian Orthodox faith and efforts to renew Christianity in Russia. In 1993 Putin's mother gave him his baptismal cross; he has never taken it off.[10] As soon as he took office, he established close relations with Patriarch Alexei II, himself a former KGB agent, but one who repented. Dimitry Pospielovsky, the noted historian of Russian Orthodoxy, told how, on Forgiveness Sunday 1991, Alexei sank to his knees and asked for forgiveness before a crowd of worshipers in the patriarchal cathedral.[11]

In a ceremony held on June 11, 2004, Putin awarded the patriarch the Order for Services to the Fatherland, First Degree. It was given for Alexei's "outstanding contribution to the strengthening of peace and accord among nations, the revival of the historical and cultural heritage of Russia, and the revival of spirituality and the strengthening of Russia."[12]

The two men, president and patriarch, worked together to bring about the union of the Russian Orthodox Church with the Russian Orthodox Church Outside Russia, thus bringing to an end a long and bitter separation. The two churches signed the Act of Canonical Communion in the Cathedral of Christ the Savior on May 17, 2007. As early as 2003, Putin had met in New York with ROCOR leaders, assuring them that the "godless regime is no longer there [in Russia]. You are sitting with a believing president."[13] This, in Solzhenitsyn's view, was another reason to support Putin, who in 2004 won reelection with 71 percent of the vote. His term ended in 2008, the year of Solzhenitsyn's death.

Before he died, however, Solzhenitsyn completed *Two Hundred Years Together*, a massive two-volume work on the often-troubled relationship between Russians and Jews. Why, many wondered, would he, so late in life, devote the better part of ten years to a subject that was certain to open him to criticism, especially from those ever ready to level accusations of anti-Semitism? Because of his unsparing depiction of Bogrov (Stolypin's assassin) and Parvus in *The Red Wheel*, he had already been labeled an anti-Semite. Why, he was asked pointedly, had he not concealed the fact that Bogrov was a Jew? In response, he told the *New York Times* that in prerevolutionary Russia "the omission of mentioning the Jewish question was considered a manifestation of anti-Semitism—and it would be unworthy for an historian of that era to pretend that that question did not exist."[14]

Still, Solzhenitsyn knew that the project would use up most of the time remaining to him, and he hoped someone else might accept the challenge. "He didn't intend to write this book at all," Alya told National Public Radio. "He was writing *The Red Wheel*. But anyone who is studying the history of the Russian Revolution will inevitably get an enormous amount of material about the role of the Jews, because it was great. Aleksandr Isaevich realized that if he put this material into *The Red Wheel* he would create the impression that he was blaming the Jews for the Russian Revolution, which he does not."[15] She did not mention the fact that she herself was Jewish on her maternal side.

The subject was, then, of critical importance, both historical and contemporary, and yet qualified researchers remained reluctant to risk their careers by taking it up. "For many years I postponed this work and would still now be pleased to avert the burden of writing it," Solzhenitsyn wrote in his introduction. "But my years are nearing their end, and I feel I must take up this task. I have never conceded to anyone the right to conceal that which *was*. Equally, I cannot call for an understanding based on an unjust portrayal of the past."[16]

In volume one, Solzhenitsyn provided a chronological account of Russian-Jewish relations, beginning with the three partitions of Poland (1772, 1793, 1795) that brought more than one million Jews under Russian rule and ending in 1916, on the eve of the February revolution. Critics pointed out that he based his history very largely on Russian-language sources, including encyclopedias. That is true. It is also true, however, that he drew upon many Jewish sources and had, as a result of his long years of work on the revolution, a profound knowledge of the pivotal events and personalities of the prerevolutionary years.

Moreover, his was not simply a straightforward re-creation of events—it was a statement of some of his most deeply held convictions. Throughout his text Solzhenitsyn made it clear that he regarded Russians and Jews as distinct nations and that national consciousness was of the utmost importance to any people; internationalism (of the communist or any other variety) or cosmopolitanism was anathema to him. When he spoke of a "nation," however, he did not mean a community of blood but of spirit.

Nor did Solzhenitsyn confuse "national" with "nationalist." He cited with approval a 1901 speech by Mark Liber (M. I. Goldman) to a congress of the "Bund" ("General Jewish Labor Bund of Lithuania, Poland and Russia"), a secular Jewish socialist party. "Until now we have been in large measure cosmopolitan. We must become national. We ought not to have any angst about this word. National does not mean nationalistic." To which Solzhenitsyn editorialized: "If only we, some 90 years later, could understand that!"[17] National was patriotic, a love of one's own land and people; nationalism was aggressive and imperialistic—unwilling or incapable of respecting the national feeling of other peoples.

Naturally, Solzhenitsyn's own national feeling, his national consciousness, was Russian, and that consciousness informs every page of volume one. Often it assumes the form of a defense, particularly with respect to the pogroms of 1881–1882 and the early years of the twentieth century that did so much damage to tsarist Russia's reputation around the world. Solzhenitsyn was quick to point out that most of the pogroms that followed in the wake of the 1881 assassination of the reformist Tsar Alexander II occurred in "New Russia" (conquered at the end of the eighteenth century), north of the Black Sea, and Ukraine—that is, not in Great Russia (Russia proper). Moreover, he disputed charges that the government incited the attacks upon Jews and Jewish property. The pogroms, he insisted, were spontaneous outbreaks of violence and the perpetrators were primarily Ukrainians, not Russians.[18]

Solzhenitsyn argued that, in general, there was far less anti-Semitism in Great Russia than in the so-called Pale of Settlement, a region in the empire's west and south that Catherine the Great created in 1791. Formerly under Polish rule, the Pale established borders outside of which permanent residency by Jews was prohibited—though over the years the government allowed more and more exceptions. "Before the entire world," Solzhenitsyn lamented, "prerevolutionary Russia—not the Empire, but *Russia*—was branded as the land of pogroms and Black Hundreds [ultra-nationalist groups of ill-repute]."[19] And yet the pogroms almost always broke out in the southwestern regions, not the heartland.

That was true of the infamous 1903 pogrom in Kishinev, then the capital of the Russian empire's province of Bessarabia (now that of Moldova). On February 9 the body of fourteen-year-old Mikhail Rybachenko was found in the nearby village of Dubossary—it contained twenty-four wounds in a clear pattern, presumed evidence of a ritual killing. Then on Holy Saturday (the day before Pascha/Easter), a Christian servant girl poisoned herself (that was not immediately known) in a Jewish hospital. A local anti-Semitic newspaper charged that the blood of both was to be used by Jews in the preparation of matzo, unleavened bread for Passover (the "blood libel"). After Divine Liturgy on Pascha, April 6 (OS), drunken rioters began to attack Jews; in three days, more than forty were murdered, some six hundred injured, and 1,300 homes and shops looted and destroyed before the authorities restored order. The timing of the first day of attacks—they occurred on Resurrection Sunday—was for Solzhenitsyn "particularly bitter and alarming."[20]

Solzhenitsyn would not and did not offer any defense of the guilty (including the negligent police), whose evil deeds left a seemingly indelible stain on subsequent Russian history. He denied, however, that the attacks were fomented from above and reported what is known—that a purported letter from Minister of the Interior Vyacheslav von Plehve to the governor of Bessarabia, ordering that the rioters be allowed free rein, was a forgery. In addition, he pointed to some of the exaggerations of violence, especially in the foreign press. One of the Hearst papers, for example, had this to say: "The massacre at Kishinev ... exceeds in naked cruelty everything that has been recorded in the annals of civilized peoples." To which Solzhenitsyn commented: "And that means also the many thousand-fold annihilated Jews in medieval Europe."[21] He added that anti-Semitism was a noted feature of life in nineteenth-century Europe—in France, Germany, and Austria-Hungary for example.

Solzhenitsyn was very far, however, from being uncritical of Russia and the Russians. The ruling theme of *Two Hundred Years Together* was, in fact, that nations, like individuals, are in perpetual need of repentance. Among the historical failings of Russians he cited "the senseless Nikon-inspired schism [and resulting persecution of Old Believers], the cruel inanities and perversities launched by Peter [the Great], and, throughout, the national shock occasioned by the zigs and zags of the post-Petrine period, a century-long squandering of Russian strength on campaigns foreign and irrelevant to the country, together with a hundred years of arrogant smugness by the nobility and a bureaucratic sclerosis for the duration of the nineteenth century."[22]

That "bureaucratic sclerosis" rendered the tsarist government incapable of dealing with its Jewish population effectively and humanely. Solzhenitsyn had no sympathy of any kind for the restrictions—including those concerning residency—imposed upon the Jews of Russia. These were, as he showed, however, anything but constant; they varied widely from tsar to tsar. On December 9, 1804, Alexander I, who was moderately tolerant of his Jewish subjects, approved a "Statute Concerning the Organization of the Jews" that had been recommended by a special committee. The statute was designed to improve the lot of Jews and mold them into "useful" citizens. To that end they were granted equal civil rights while their children gained the right to attend elementary schools, gymnasia, and universities. In villages large and small, however, complicated occupational restrictions applied, the most painful of which was that with regard to taverns and inns and the selling of liquor—a traditional occupation among Jews; and in the last years of Alexander I's rule, the government lengthened the list of prohibitions.

Under Nicholas I, an unabashed anti-Semite, the Jews' situation worsened. Most notably, the tsar ordered that males between twelve and twenty-five be conscripted for a period of twenty-five years (later reduced to five to ten years). Naturally, many of those liable for service fled. Nicholas did approve a new statute in 1835 that replaced that of 1804, confirmed all rights of the

Jewish religion, and permitted the Jews to practice any trade with the same rights as any other subject of the crown—though only within the Pale of Settlement. Solzhenitsyn concluded that "the sudden death of the tsar [in 1855] liberated the Jews from an oppressive time exactly as the death of Stalin did a century later."[23]

Alexander II (the "Tsar Liberator") presided over an age of reform, highlighted by the emancipation of the serfs in 1861.[24] In part because of the dramatic growth in Russia's Jewish population—by 1880 it represented 51 percent of world Jewry—the tsar was determined to solve the "Jewish question" by merging Jews with the general population; that is, he hoped to Russify them. He and his government, Solzhenitsyn wrote, believed that the Jews' isolation could be overcome by means of a "common education." And in fact, increasing numbers of Jews were attending Russian universities. By 1881, 9 percent of university students were Jewish—and in the medical and legal faculties the percentage was much higher. But almost all of those students came from the bourgeoisie or intelligentsia; the broad masses of Jews remained in Jewish schools, isolated not only from Russian society but from the Jewish intelligentsia. What this meant, Solzhenitsyn wrote, is that Russian Jewry had reached a "watershed between a cosmopolitan and a national course."[25]

The granting of full legal equality to Jews might have decided the issue, and when the tsar appointed the liberal Mikhail Loris-Melikov minister of the interior in 1880, Jews hoped that their day had finally arrived. On March 1, 1881, however, terrorist members of the People's Will assassinated Alexander II, and as Solzhenitsyn wrote, "with one blow brought the movement for full equality of the Jews to a standstill."[26]

The accession of Alexander III brought new and often terrifying persecutions of the Jews. Solzhenitsyn doubted, however, that the tsar ever said, "I must admit that it pleases me when one thrashes a Jew."[27] In fact, there is no evidence that he personally ordered any of the pogroms that followed in the wake of his father's murder. Nevertheless, the multiple pogroms of the early 1880s left their mark on educated Jews. "They no longer hoped," Solzhenitsyn wrote, "for a complete merging with the land of Russia and its inhabitants." At the same time, a governmental "Jewish Committee" reached the conclusion that "the goal of merging the Jews with the broader population, which the government has pursued over the last 25 years, is unattainable."[28]

With that in mind, perhaps, Minister of the Interior Nikolai Ignatyev proposed, and Alexander III enacted, the supposedly temporary "May Laws" (May

3, 1882) that prohibited Jews in the Pale of Settlement from settling outside of towns and boroughs or transacting business on Sundays or Orthodox Feast Days. The laws did not apply to Jews in existing agricultural colonies or to physicians, attorneys, and engineers. Still, the worsening atmosphere prompted an historic Jewish emigration (mostly from Poland, Lithuania, and White Russia) to the United States.

That did not sit well with Alexander III. And neither did the fact that so many Jews participated in the revolutionary movement. In 1887, after years of reflection and irresolution, the tsar resolved to suppress the Jews by legal and political means at his disposal.[29] Convinced that gymnasia and universities were breeding grounds for revolution, the government established admission quotas for Jews: 10 percent in the Pale of Settlement, 5 percent outside the Pale, and 3 percent in Moscow and St. Petersburg.

Solzhenitsyn was quick to point out that the quota allowed for many exceptions. It did not apply, for example, to gymnasia for girls. "In Rostov's Andrejeva-Lyzeum, where my mother went to school," he wrote, "Jewish girls comprised more than half of the class."[30] Nor did the quota apply in such special schools as the Moscow Academy for Painting, Architecture, and Sculpture or the Petersburg School for Psychology and Neurology. Private schools, too, were exempt from the restrictive admission regulations. Nevertheless, the percentage of Jews enrolled in Russian universities did decline significantly, and this occasioned much bitterness and anger.

On the death of Alexander III, his son ascended the throne as Nicholas II, fated to be the last Russian tsar. Nicholas was no friend of the Jews, and during his reign there were a great many pogroms, including those in Kishinev and Odessa—and these led to Jewish emigration on a large scale. In December 1906 the recently appointed prime minister, Pyotr Stolypin, presented a proposal for a significant lifting of restrictions on Jews of such a nature that it would pave the way to full equality of rights; unfortunately the proposal was not acted upon. Granting the Jews full equality of rights might have had the effect of keeping those not already imbued with the spirit of rebellion away from revolutionary parties.

Looking back upon the course of more than a century, Solzhenitsyn concluded that "the regime proved incapable of solving the problem of its Jewish population, neither offering an acceptable form of assimilation nor allowing the Jews to remain in the kind of voluntary isolation that had prevailed a century earlier when they were first incorporated into the empire." The three decades between the 1870s and the turn of the century had witnessed a flowering of intellectual energy among the Jewish elite, whose members felt hemmed in not only by the Pale of Settlement but by the Russian empire. That should be kept in mind, "when focusing on the specific ways in which Russian Jews were denied equal rights, on the Pale of Settlement, and on the restrictive quotas in various fields of endeavor."[31] These "*repressions* and *restrictions* were indeed irksome, painful, and atrociously unjust."[32]

In the first volume of *Two Hundred Years Together,* Solzhenitsyn defended Russians and the tsarist government when, in his opinion, the charges leveled against them were either false or overdrawn, but his overall judgment of their treatment of the Jews was severe. That did not mean that the Russian *nation,* as such, was guilty of the wrongs done; it did mean that no nation "can shirk its responsibility for its members. As nations, we contribute to their formation." There was a pressing need, therefore, for *national* repentance along with an effort to recapture "the spiritual strength and purity that earlier in our history had flowed from St. Sergius of Radonezh [c. 1314–1392]."[33] St. Sergius was the father of northern Russian monasticism and founder of Holy Trinity (later Holy Trinity-St. Sergius) Lavra (Monastery), the very symbol of Russian Orthodoxy. Solzhenitsyn was drawn to St. Sergius by his ascetic life, which, not incidentally, included strenuous physical labor.

Solzhenitsyn pointed out that the Jews, like the Russians, comprised a *nation,* one of the world's most united in spirit. For centuries Judaism had formed the basis of Jewish national consciousness, but during the nineteenth century, as Russia's Jews became increasingly secular in outlook, they, or rather their "Enlightened" elite, experienced a dizzying back and forth between loss and recovery of the national consciousness. The *Haskala* (Jewish Enlightenment) had arrived in Russia from Germany by the 1840s, bringing with it German culture; "the Russian language," Solzhenitsyn observed, "remained foreign to its adherents (they knew Goethe and Schiller, but not Pushkin and Lermontov)."[34]

That, however, began to change during the age of the Great Reforms. By the end of the 1870s, the members of the secularized elite were learning Russian and beginning to participate in Russian cultural and political life—among the *maskilim* (the Enlightened), the process of accommodation with all things Russian developed rapidly. Solzhenitsyn cited one of them: "There is no Jewish nation. The Jews regard themselves as Russians of the Mosaic faith. The Jews are aware that their deliverance consists of fusion with the Russian people."[35] This was music to the ears of government leaders, though they knew that the Jewish masses remained alienated from Russian society and the Jewish intelligentsia.

The assassination of Alexander II and the pogroms of 1881–1882 dampened Jewish enthusiasm for assimilation, but it did not end it, especially among those Jews who enlisted in the revolutionary movement—still Populist (and hence for the peasantry) but awakening to Marxism (and hence for the proletariat). Fascinated by the ideas they discovered in the writings of Russian liberals such as Ivan Turgenev and radicals such as Vissarion Belinsky and Nikolai Dobrolyubov, they turned away from their Jewishness. In the back of their minds, however, was the hope that the revolutionary liberation of the Russian people would, at the same time, lead to the liberation of the other peoples of the empire, including the Jews.

The decade of the 1880s witnessed the decline of Populism, a movement in which Jews played a minor role, and the rise of a Marxist alternative. As he did regularly throughout *Two Hundred Years Together*, Solzhenitsyn turned to Jewish writers—in this case to help explain why Jews were particularly drawn to the latter. One wrote that Jewish thinking was essentially rationalistic and hence "receptive to doctrines such as revolutionary Marxism." Another pointed out that Marxism was imported from Germany and that Russian Jews learned socialist theory from German books.[36] Lenin, as leader of the Bolshevik faction of the Russian Social Democratic Workers' Party (Marxist), insisted that the Party's Jewish members assimilate and cease being Jews. "In his superficial and absurd internationalism," Solzhenitsyn commented, "[Lenin] failed to grasp the profound and historical rootedness of the Jewish question."[37]

That was true even though one of Lenin's earliest and closest comrades was consciously Jewish: Yuli Tsederbaum, who adopted the revolutionary name Julius (or L.) Martov. Before cooperating with Lenin in the 1898 founding of the Social Democratic Workers' Party, Martov helped to lay the ideological and organizational foundations for the "Bund," founded in Vilna in 1897. The following year the Bund became a collective member of the Social Democratic Party; in 1903, after the Party split into Bolshevik and Menshevik factions, the Bund generally sided with Martov and other Mensheviks who argued for a mass party, not, as Lenin insisted, a party limited to professional revolutionaries.

The Bund's relations with Lenin's Bolsheviks could only be difficult. Our goal, Lenin maintained, should be to drive out the Bund; "the Russian party must be

Russian."[38] Zionism, though socialist, was still worse. According to Bolsheviks, it was a reactionary movement, a "party of despairing, hopeless pessimism."[39] Solzhenitsyn emphasized that Russian Zionism preceded the publication of Theodor Herzl's famous Der Judenstaat (The Jewish State, 1896). At the end of the 1860s, the Russian-Jewish novelist Peretz Smolenskin (who wrote in Hebrew), having rejected assimilation, promoted the idea of Jewish nationhood—Jewry was, he insisted, "a nation, not a religious community of belief."[40]

Even more important was the work of Achad Ha'am (b. Asher Ginsberg to a family of Hasidim—a form of mysticism). In 1889 Ha'am founded the "Zionist League" (Bene Mosheh, or Sons of Moses), the manifesto of which spoke of "the primacy of national over religious consciousness and the subordination of personal to national interest." Opposed to Herzl's political Zionism, which he judged to be "alienated from the spiritual values of Jewish culture and tradition," Ha'am favored a "moral Zionism" located in Palestine.[41] This was probably as close to traditional Jewry as any Zionist could be. By 1905, according to Solzhenitsyn, traditional Jewry had "lost an entire generation to Zionism, worldly liberalism, Enlightened conservatism (less often), and—most portentous—the revolutionary movement."[42]

That young Jews were attracted to "worldly liberalism" was evidenced by the fact that they forged a close association with the Kadets. In the Pale of Settlement the Jews constituted a large majority of Party members and in Russia proper the second largest national group. For the Kadets, we know, Solzhenitsyn reserved a special contempt. He had even more contempt for the press—freed from censorship in 1905—which aligned itself with liberal and radical parties and movements. In fact, editors and correspondents, the most important of whom were Jews, "displayed an unconcealed sympathy for terror and revolution."[43]

Enlisting in the revolutionary movement and embracing Zionism were, then, among the options for Russia's Jews, but there were others. They could retain their religious identity and self-isolation (an option that was rapidly losing its appeal); they could assimilate or emigrate. But their best choice, in Solzhenitsyn's judgment, was to struggle for cultural and national autonomy "with the goal of an active but separate existence in the country." The Jews, he wrote, would do well to remember the wise counsel of the prophet Jeremiah to the Jews taken to Babylon: "And seek the peace of the city whither I have caused you to be carried away captives, and pray unto the Lord for it: for in the peace thereof shall ye have peace" (Jeremiah 29:7).[44]

In a chapter on Jewish and Russian national consciousness prior to World War I, Solzhenitsyn called attention to a forgotten polemical article of 1909 by Pyotr Struve. With unblinking honesty, Struve defended national consciousness. Each nationality, he wrote, was attracted to and repulsed by particular nations, feelings for which they could not always cite reasons. What was required of nations was not that they deny those feelings, but that they not allow them to deny other nations equal standing before the law. Should, then, Russia's Jews have equal rights? Yes, naturally, Struve wrote.

Various strata of the Russian nation, Struve continued, would nevertheless continue to feel alienated from Jews (just as Zionists felt alienated from Russians). It did Russians little good, he concluded, to disguise their national feelings. "All [of us Russians] have a right to these feelings. The clearer that is understood, the fewer misunderstandings there will be in the future."[45]

Struve's article stirred up a hornet's nest, but the author did not shy away from replying to a critique by Pavel Milyukov. "This shocking 'a-Semitism' is a far more propitious basis for a just solution of the Jewish question than an inexpedient battle of 'anti-Semitism' against 'philo-Semitism.' None of the non-Russian nationalities love all Russians unconditionally or even pretend to do so. 'A-Semitism' combined with a clear and sensible understanding of certain moral and political principles (and state necessities) is for our Jewish fellow citizens far more necessary and advantageous than a sentimental 'philo-Semitism,' or special pleading." (To which the editor added that the journal believed in "the recognition of the particularities of each nationality and respect for them.")[46]

Solzhenitsyn left his readers in little doubt that this was also his view of the Russian and Jewish nations and the proper relationship between the two. At the same time he made clear his undying opposition to internationalism and cosmopolitanism. Let each nation look within itself and not to some abstract "international community"—or some other nation—for historical and existential direction. The Jews, he wrote, may not have gained equality of rights under the tsars, but the power of their development, their grievances, and their abilities found a place in Russians' social consciousness. "We accepted their view of our history and the way out of [its dilemmas]." To understand that, according to Solzhenitsyn, was more important than to calculate what percentage of Jews participated in the revolutionary movement or in Bolshevik power.[47]

Solzhenitsyn devoted the second volume of *Two Hundred Years Together* to a historical-spiritual study of the relationship between Russians and Jews under Soviet rule. Within that context he called upon both nations to accept responsibility for past actions. If that meant that some would charge him with anti-Semitism, he was prepared to defend himself. "At no point," he wrote, "have I had the feeling that I was hostile to the Jews. I wrote with more sympathy about the Jews than many Jews have displayed when writing about Russians." His aim in writing the book, he said, was to promote mutual understanding between the two peoples, which could only be achieved by calling things, especially iniquitous things, by their proper names. "It appears to be evident that the truth concerning our common past, for the Jews as well as for the Russians, is *morally necessary*."[48]

Of the February revolution, the subject of his first chapter, Solzhenitsyn had, as we know, nothing good to report. While it disturbed him that many Jews welcomed the collapse of tsarist rule and supported the Provisional Government, he could understand their enthusiasm for a regime that removed all legal restrictions that had been placed upon them. More important, he insisted that it was not the Jews who brought revolutionary ruin down upon the Russians. "We ourselves brought about this catastrophe—our God-anointed tsar, the court circle, the talentless Generals, the ossified bureaucracy; and with them their opponents—the elitist intelligentsia, the Octobrists, the members of the zemstvos, the Constitutional Democrats (Kadets), the revolutionary democrats, the socialists and revolutionaries.... Precisely *these* brought us to ruin."[49]

During the few months in 1917 that the Provisional Government claimed to rule Russia, real power rested in the hands of the Petrograd Soviet of Workers' and Soldiers' Deputies, especially its executive committee. As the Petrograd Soviet expanded to include representatives from other areas of Russia, it rechristened itself the All-Russian Soviet of Workers' and Soldiers' Deputies, headed by an All-Russian Central Executive Committee. The members of the Soviet were primarily Mensheviks and Social Revolutionaries, parties to which socialist Jews were primarily drawn. By September 1917, however, the Bolsheviks had gained a majority in the Soviet, and Leon Trotsky (Lev Bronstein), a thirty-seven-year-old Jew from Ukraine, was chairman; he quickly transformed the Soviet into an arm of the Bolshevik Party and engineered the Bolsheviks' October coup d'état. Nevertheless, Solzhenitsyn pointed out that most Jewish socialists opposed the Bolsheviks and were not responsible for the coup that brought Lenin and Trotsky to power.

Not the least of the reasons for the Jews' lack of culpability for the October seizure of power was that they had already gained their freedom as a result of the February revolution. Once the Bolsheviks were in power, however, secular Jews became activists on their behalf—and in the process achieved high-ranking positions. In addition to Trotsky, an internationalist whose closest comrades were Jews, there were Yakov Sverdlov (chairman of the Central Executive Committee of the Congress of Soviets), Grigory Zinoviev (Apfelbaum; head of the Petrograd city and regional government), and Lev Kamenev (Rozenfeld; chairman of the Moscow Soviet and deputy chairman of the Council of People's Commissars). Solzhenitsyn identified many more by name and position of authority.[50]

According to Solzhenitsyn these men were not Jews in spirit; they were renegades. He asked, however, whether or not a nation should "preserve a memory of the fiends and demons that it engendered" and answered his own question: "*We must remember.* Every people must remember them as *its own.*" Not only that but they must answer for them, "just as we would answer for members of our own family." The Jewish nation had therefore to answer for its renegades, not "to other peoples, but to oneself, to one's consciousness, and to God"—just as Russians had to answer for the sins of its renegades. In that regard Solzhenitsyn instanced Lenin, of mixed ethnicity and a despiser of Russia and Russian Orthodoxy, who was nevertheless Russian. And "it was we Russians who brought into being the social environment in which Lenin grew and filled with hate. It was *in us* that the weakening of the Orthodox faith took place, that faith in which he could have matured instead of trying to destroy it."[51]

Among the crimes committed by renegade Jews, Solzhenitsyn listed the major role they played in the July 17, 1918, murder of Tsar Nicholas II and his family in Yekaterinburg's euphemistically named "House of Special Purpose." According to Dmitri Volkogonov, "It is inconceivable that the action could have been carried out without the sanction . . . of Lenin personally."[52] The execution order was, however, signed by Sverdlov and taken to Yekaterinburg by his close friend Filipp Goloshchekin, a Jew who was commissar of the Urals Military District. The commander of the execution squad, Yakov Yurovsky, was a baptized Jew.

Then there was the matter of membership in the Cheka (political police). In Ukraine, for example, Feliks Dzerzhinsky placed Jews in seven of the ten top positions and saw to it that Jews made up nearly 80 percent of the rank-and-file agents. Among the leading investigators in the division for the combating of counterrevolution—the most important division of the Cheka—fully half were Jews.[53] As Leonard Schapiro once wrote, "Anyone who had the misfortune to fall into the hands of the Cheka stood a very good chance of finding himself confronted with and possibly shot by a Jewish investigator."[54] So ubiquitous were Jews among the political police that Reds, Whites, and the general population gained the impression that Chekists and Jews were one and the same.

Why, Solzhenitsyn asked, did so many Jews, whose religion was so much at odds with godless Bolshevism, participate in the movement? Was it because of the oppression they had suffered in the past? Solzhenitsyn did not think so. One should remember, he pointed out, that there were, at almost the same time as the Bolshevik revolution, communist revolutions in Bavaria and Hungary in which the number of Jewish participants was large; in neither land did the Jews suffer oppression.

In Hungary "the legal status of Jews was excellent; legal restrictions had not existed for them for a long time." On the contrary, they occupied leading positions in cultural and economic life.[55] Nevertheless the principal leaders of the short-lived Hungarian Soviet Republic of 1919 included Béla Kun (Kohn), commissar of foreign affairs; Tibor Szamuely, organizer of the Red Terror; György Lukács, cultural dictator; and Jenő Varga, principal economic adviser. All were of Jewish origin. Why so many Jews embraced Bolshevism might never be known, but of one thing Solzhenitsyn was certain—self-justification would lower the level of the Jews' self-understanding or destroy it altogether.

Having said that, Solzhenitsyn was quick to point out that significant numbers of Jews refused to embrace Bolshevism. "Rabbis, unsalaried university lecturers, renowned physicians, and the great mass of average citizens gave the Bolsheviks the cold shoulder."[56] Among them, he was eager to call attention to a neglected hero of the anti-Bolshevik underground—Aleksandr Abramovich Vilenkin. In the underground and in prison, Vilenkin inspired resistance in others before being shot by the Cheka. The murderous head of the Petrograd Cheka, Moisei Uritsky, was assassinated by Leonid Kannegisser, a Jew. A few days later, August 30, 1918, another Jew, Fanya Kaplan, shot and almost killed Lenin.

Still, because Jews had become so identified with the Bolshevik government, the savage civil war (1918–1921) witnessed an eruption of pogroms, especially in chaotic Ukraine, where Ukrainians, Reds, Whites, and anarchists vied for power. "In their breadth, scope, and cruelty," Solzhenitsyn wrote, "these pogroms outstripped beyond measure" those in 1881–1882, 1903, and 1905.[57] The greatest—but not the sole—responsibility for the pogroms belonged to the so-called Directory, a revolutionary committee of the Ukrainian People's Republic led by Volodimir Vinnichenko and Symon Petliura, a socialist and Ukrainian nationalist, who had once studied for the priesthood. Petliura's armed forces murdered an estimated 50,000 Jews, among whom were four-teen members of the family of Sholom Schwartzbard, who, on May 25, 1926, gunned Petliura down on a Paris street.

Although the Volunteer Army of Whites was not initially anti-Semitic, by 1919 its members had become convinced that *all* Jews sided with the Reds. Moreover, so widespread was anti-Semitism in Ukraine that it seemed a means of increasing support for the White cause. Pogroms carried out by the Volunteer Army under General Anton Denikin's command "became coldly calculated incidents of wholesale rape, extreme brutality, and unprecedented destruction." In September 1919 Denikin's forces conducted a five-day pogrom during which they murdered 1,500–2,000 Jews.[58] As Winston Churchill warned Denikin, those atrocities made it difficult to rally support for the White cause; they cer-tainly contributed to the Red victory.

During the 1920s, according to Solzhenitsyn, Russian Jews served the Bolshevik regime without foreseeing the consequences for themselves. One of the Soviets' pet ideas at the time, for example, was the creation of agricultural colonies for Jews. Initially the plan called for the resettlement of 100,000 Jewish families in southern Ukraine and northern Crimea, but relatively few families responded with enthusiasm; what is more, the Crimean Tatars took a dim view of the idea. The program therefore proved to be unsuccessful. Equally unsuccessful, at least in the beginning, was the 1927 plan to create an autonomous Jewish region centered at Birobidzhan, on the inhospitable Chinese border. As Solzhenitsyn pointed out, most Jews who settled there soon left.

What Soviet leaders had primarily in mind was a counterweight to Zionist aspirations for a Jewish homeland. For much the same reason, the regime for-bade any encouragement of Hebraic culture, which it regarded as the carrier of religion as well as Zionism; the goal was to create a *Soviet* (secular) culture in the Yiddish language. The authorities encouraged Yiddish literature so long as it helped to separate readers from the Jews' history—their national spirit and tradition. By promoting internationalism and atheism, Yiddish writers could help create *Soviet* men and women.

Lenin never recovered fully from the attempt on his life made by Fanya Kaplan. Even before he died in January 1924, therefore, the struggle for power between the Jewish Trotsky and the Georgian Stalin had begun. As it turned out, it was a mismatch; in 1929 Stalin consolidated all power in his hands and expelled his rival from Soviet soil. Although the *Vozhd* (Leader) seems always to have felt an aversion to Jews, the official Soviet atmosphere in the 1930s was, according to Solzhenitsyn, "quite free of animosity toward the Jews," at least toward those—the majority—who sympathized with the regime.[59]

"There is no doubt," Yuri Slezkine has written, "that the Jews had a much higher proportion of elite members than any other ethnic group in the USSR."[60] Among Jews who occupied positions of power in the mid-1930s were Maxim Litvinov (b. Meir Wallach-Finkelstein), people's commissar for foreign affairs; Lazar Kaganovich, people's commissar for transport; and Genrikh Yagoda (b. Yenokh Iyeguda), people's commissar for internal affairs (that is, director of the NKVD).

Yagoda was not alone. The NKVD, according to Slezkine, "was one of the most Jewish of all Soviet institutions. In January 1937, on the eve of the Great Terror, the 111 top NKVD officials included forty-two Jews, thirty-five Russians, eight Latvians, and twenty-six others. Out of twenty NKVD directorates, twelve (60 percent, including state security, police, labor camps, and resettlement [deportations]) were headed by officers who identified themselves as ethnic Jews."[61] Solzhenitsyn called particular attention to Naum Eitingon, who recruited Ramón Mercader to assassinate Trotsky in 1940. Based upon the post-Soviet research of others, he also reported the story of NKVD official Isaï Davidovich Berg, who in 1937—that is, before the Nazis began to gas millions of Jews—designed a means to gas those on their way to be shot by directing exhaust fumes into a "gas van."[62]

Because he had identified Jewish GULag chiefs in *The GULag Archipelago*, Solzhenitsyn restricted himself to mentioning only a few, such as Lazar Kogan and Israel Pliner, in *Two Hundred Years Together*; he did not neglect to report that both men were shot in 1939.[63] Whatever their offense—if there was any—it was not that they had clung to their identity as Jews; they knew that Stalin was determined to stamp out any sign of Jewish tradition. The attempt in the 1920s to create a "Living Synagogue" (modeled on the "Living Church") having failed, the regime closed 257 synagogues (57 percent of those that had existed in the 1920s) at the end of the 1930s. Those that remained open often had to function without a rabbi, most of whom (there being few "Red rabbis") the police arrested in 1937–1938.

At the same time that Stalin closed synagogues and arrested rabbis, he began a brutal repression of Orthodox believers, including the closing of some ten thousand churches, many of which were destroyed. Among the latter was Moscow's Cathedral of Christ the Savior, dynamited in 1931 to make way for a Palace of the Soviets, a planned monument to socialism topped with a statue of Lenin 164 feet high; due to construction problems and a lack of funds, the palace was never built. The destruction of churches served a dual purpose—it was at once an attack on Christianity and on the Russian nation. At the sixteenth Party congress in 1930, Stalin called for an "energetic fight against chauvinism— *particularly Great Russian chauvinism.*"[64]

In his chapter on the war with Germany, Solzhenitsyn displayed a particular sympathy for Russia's Jews, not least because of his memories of Jewish comrades in military service. "Among them," he wrote, "were courageous men. I cannot fail to mention two particularly fearless men who served in the anti-tank units: my university friend Lieutenant Emmanuel Masin and Boris Gammerov, a young student called to arms (both suffered wounds)." (We recall that it was Gammerov who, when the two men met in Butyrka prison, stunned Solzhenitsyn by professing a belief in God.) Solzhenitsyn also singled out for praise two Jews in the division he commanded, a fellow officer, and his friend Lev Kopelev.[65] The actual number of Jews who served in the Red Army or in partisan units during the war is uncertain, but best estimates place it at about five hundred thousand.

Many thousands of these Jewish combatants sacrificed their lives in the struggle against the German invaders, but as the world now knows, the Nazis murdered far more. As Solzhenitsyn wrote, the mass murders of Jews and commissars ("bearers of the Jewish-Bolshevist Weltanschauung") began in the first days of the invasion in June 1941. He provided numbers of victims in several occupied cities before turning his attention to Kiev. As Vasily Grossman, then a war correspondent, wrote at the time: "People who had come from Kiev told me that the Germans had surrounded with a ring of troops a huge mass grave in which bodies of 50,000 Jews killed in Kiev in the autumn of 1941 were buried."[66]

On September 27 Major General Kurt Eberhard (military governor of Kiev) and Friedrich Jeckeln (higher SS and police leader) posted orders that the Jews of Kiev prepare for "evacuation" by gathering up identity papers, money and valuables, and warm clothing. Over thirty-three thousand Jews reported and, not knowing that death awaited them, were transported to the ravine at Babi Yar. There a special commando unit of the SS ordered its prisoners to hand over their valuables and strip naked.[67] Over two days, September 29 and 30, the members of the unit shot and killed 33,771 Jews; later they used the same location to murder thousands more Jews, Romanis, and Ukrainian nationalists. The murders at Babi Yar, Solzhenitsyn wrote, "shock precisely because of the cold-blooded calculation, the business-like organization, which are so typical for the twentieth century—the crown of humanistic civilization."[68]

Based upon recent (1990s) archival research carried out by others, Solzhenitsyn set the number of Soviet Jews who perished within the 1945 borders and between 1941 and 1945 at 2,733,000. Not all were victims of planned mass murder, but those who were added to the generally recognized number of six million victims of the Shoah or Holocaust. On this latter subject Solzhenitsyn had things to say that he certainly knew would occasion controversy. He cited numerous Jewish authors who recorded—or themselves took—very different views of the Shoah. For many it was proof that God was dead. Others held that in the death camps a new Torah had been given that the Jews had not yet learned to read. Still others condemned the Western world for having turned its back on them.[69]

Solzhenitsyn cited contemporary Israelis who warned against a Jewish preoccupation with the Shoah. According to one, the Shoah had become the *ideology* of the Jewish state, a state cult. In a similar vein another Israeli author wrote that "the cult of the Shoah had filled the void in the souls of non-religious Jews" and cautioned that "if we do not recover from the trauma of Auschwitz, we will never become a normal people." Still another Israeli, a historian, testified that he did not hold evil "goyim" responsible for the Jews' misfortunes; nor did he regard the Jews as unfortunate little lambs or playthings in foreign hands. "The terrible catastrophe," he concluded, "was not only the result of wicked plans of the ene-mies of humanity, but also the fatal miscalculations of the Jews themselves, of their leaders and activists."[70]

Other Jewish commentators went further. According to one (Dan Levin), "The Shoah was to a great extent a punishment for sins, among others the sin of leadership in the communist movement." Another argued that the Shoah and the feelings of sympathy it evoked around the world had resulted in a will-ingness to excuse Jews for sins that were unpardonable in others. Still another maintained that the moral capital the Jews gained from the Shoah had been spent and that the world had every right to treat the Jews as they would any other people.

At the very least, Solzhenitsyn himself believed that the Jews should reflect not only upon their sufferings but upon the relation those sufferings might bear to their sins. The Russians who, during the war, suffered death, starvation, and destruction on a massive scale, would likewise do well to reflect upon *their* sins—"from the cruel and inhuman period of the Revolution through the cowed indifference of the Soviet era to the thievish repulsiveness of the post-Soviet epoch. In the unbearable recognition that in this century we Russians have rav-aged our own history ... we should ask 'have we not here to do with punish-ment from a higher Authority?'"[71]

It was, then, Solzhenitsyn's conviction that the sufferings experienced by Jews and Russians in the twentieth century were, to an uncertain degree, the conse-quence of national sins. We recall that as he was recovering from cancer surgery in the GULag, he was visited by Dr. Boris Nikolayevich Kornfeld, who spoke of his conversion from Judaism to Christianity—and of something else. "I have become convinced," the doctor told Solzhenitsyn, "that there is no punishment that comes to us in this life on earth which is undeserved. Superficially it can have nothing to do with what we are guilty of in actual fact, but if you go over your life with a fine-tooth comb and ponder it deeply, you will always be able to hunt down that transgression of yours for which you have now received this blow."[72]

Solzhenitsyn wrote that those words struck a chord in him and that "I accept [them] quite completely *for myself*"—but not before he puzzled over the fact that GULag torturers seemed to escape punishment. It was then that he concluded that the meaning of earthly existence lay "in the development of the soul." From *that* point of view, the torturers *had* been punished—their souls were utterly corrupted. More obvious punishment was "inflicted on those whose develop-ment ... *holds out hope*."[73]

The years extending from the end of the war to Stalin's death in 1953 constituted a time of troubles for Soviet Jews, although things began promisingly enough. Throughout 1947 the *Vozhd* backed the idea of an independent Jewish state in Palestine and, within two days after the May 15, 1948, founding of the state of Israel, granted Soviet recognition while condemning the Arab armies' invasion. Soon, however, it dawned on him that his support of Israel had heightened national self-consciousness among Soviet Jews.[74]

Stalin, therefore, turned on the Jewish Anti-Fascist Committee (JAC) that he himself had called into existence in April 1942 in order to rally political and material support in the West for the Soviet war effort. In January 1948 he ordered the murder of Solomon Mikhoels, the actor and director of the Moscow State Jewish Theater, who served as chairman of the JAC and who had suggested that a Jewish republic be established in the Crimea. In Minsk, where he was judging plays for the Stalin Prize Committee, the MGB took him to Belorussian boss Lavrenti Tsanava's dacha where he was probably injected with poison, beaten, and shot. The killers then took his body into town and ran over it with a truck.[75] By 1952 almost all members of the JAC—about seventy in number—had been arrested and executed.

Beginning in January 1949 with a campaign against "an anti-patriotic" group of theater critics, most of them Jews, Stalin launched a wider campaign against "cosmopolitans," that is Jews. The police did not arrest those so identified, but the leading ideological, scientific, and cultural institutions and publications drove them from their midst. But worse was to come. On January 13, 1953, *Pravda* and *Izvestiya* announced that nine doctors, six of whom were Jews, had been arrested and charged with poisoning Andrei Zhdanov, the postwar cultural enforcer, and plotting the murder of other high-ranking officials. To obtain confessions, according to Khrushchev, Stalin issued orders to "beat, beat and beat again."[76] Fortunately, the dictator died on March 5 and very soon after *Pravda* reported that a reexamination of the case proved the charges to be false; those who survived the "investigation" were released.

After a brief struggle for power, Nikita Khrushchev assumed leadership of the Soviet Union in 1953 and ushered in an era of relative relaxation with respect to the Jews. It was not, according to Solzhenitsyn, that the new dictator had any particular love for Jews—he was in fact a fanatical anti-Semite—but he knew that anti-Jewish policies would tarnish his image abroad.[77] At the same time, however, he was as intolerant of Judaism as he was of Orthodox Christianity, and his regime closed a great many synagogues. Moreover the Suez Crisis of 1956—during which Israel, Britain, and France attempted to force a reopening of the Suez Canal, which Egyptian president Gamal Abdel Nasser had nationalized—prompted him to open an offensive against Zionism.

The same crisis and Khrushchev's response to it intensified Soviet Jews' national self-consciousness and feelings of solidarity with Israel. As the fifties gave way to the sixties, Jewishness, even among non-Jews, became almost chic. "The Jewish theme was taken up in samizdat [self-published typescripts circulated from hand to hand] and expressed in poetry evenings which were much loved by young people.... Yevgeni Yevtushenko appropriated the new trend and in his poem 'Babi Yar' [1961] declared himself to be a Jew in spirit."[78] Although he had always stirred controversy—he managed to speak both for dissent and for the established order—Yevtushenko became for a time a spokesman for post-Stalinist Soviet youth. He often, for example, recited publicly his most famous poem—always to thunderous applause.

Dmitri Shostakovich was another Soviet cultural figure who felt drawn to the Jewish theme, and in 1962 he composed his Symphony No. 13, subtitled "Babi Yar." The choral symphony is a setting of five of Yevtushenko's poems, the first and most important of which is "Babi Yar"—both powerful and haunting. Party leaders took a dim view of the work, not least because they preferred to emphasize the loss of life of all Soviet citizens, rather than focus on the sufferings of Jews alone. At the first performance, in Moscow on December 18, 1962, no one occupied the government box. Taking their cue from the authorities, critics ignored the work, but audiences acclaimed it. "Babi Yar," Solzhenitsyn concluded, "had for Jewry, and not only Soviet Jewry, the force of an animating and healing ray."[79]

As their feelings of national—that is, Jewish—solidarity deepened, Soviet Jews became ever more alienated from Russians. Solzhenitsyn cited the case of Natan Sharansky who, after emigrating to Israel, became a cabinet minister and writer. Shortly after arriving in his new home, Sharansky wrote that "our family was indeed assimilated, but nevertheless Jewish." After the Six-Day War of 1967, he continued, "I suddenly perceived a clear difference between me and the non-Jews around me, the feeling of a fundamental dissimilarity between my Jewish consciousness and the national consciousness of Russians."[80]

There is no doubt that Israel's stunning victory over Syria, Jordan, and Egypt in the Six-Day War awakened in Soviet Jews profound feelings of pride and a deepening of national self-consciousness. "I sat at my dacha glued to the radio, rejoicing and celebrating," remembered Mikhail Agursky, a contributor to *From Under the Rubble.* "The Six-Day War convinced me that my platonic Zionism was becoming the real thing and that, sooner rather than later, I was fated to live in Israel."[81] Much to the displeasure of Soviet leaders, large numbers of Jews began to apply for emigration visas. Only a small number were granted permission to leave; those who were refused, usually for "national security" reasons, became known as "refuseniks."

Determined to make their escape, sixteen refuseniks, organized by Eduard Kuznetsov and Mark Dymshits (a former military pilot), plotted to seize a small aircraft scheduled to fly from Leningrad to Priozersk, with a stopover at Smolnoye. On June 15, 1970, they purchased all tickets on the 12-seater and planned to force the pilots off the plane at the Smolnoye airport. Instead, the MVD (Ministry of Internal Affairs) arrested them when the plane landed. At the December 1970 trial, the court sentenced Kuznetsov and Dymshits to death and the others to periods of four to fifteen years in prison. Thanks to an appeal from US President Richard Nixon and other world leaders, the Soviets reduced the death sentences to fifteen years; in 1979 they were exchanged for two Soviet spies who had been arrested in the United States. According to Solzhenitsyn, the trial "can be considered a historical turning point in the destiny of Soviet Jewry."[82]

Now fully aware of the threat posed by the Jews' reawakening national consciousness, the Soviet regime stepped up its anti-Zionist campaign and increased Jewish disabilities in employment and education—which in turn alienated the Jews even further from communism. That was all well and good according to Solzhenitsyn but where, he asked, was the Jews' sense of moral responsibility—their repentance—for their former support of and leadership roles in the Bolshevik regime? At the same time he again made it clear that the Russians had a duty to confront *their* sins of the past. "We will never weary of calling Russians to repentance; without repentance we will have no future."[83]

Solzhenitsyn likened the exodus of the Jews from the Soviet Union in the seventies and eighties to their famed exodus from ancient Egypt. He cited the book of Exodus 5:1: "Moses and Aaron went in, and told Pharaoh, Thus saith the Lord God of Israel, Let my people go." Similarly, the refuseniks demanded that the Soviet leaders let their people go, and under pressure from America and Europe they soon did. In 1971 thirteen thousand Jews emigrated (98 percent to Israel); in 1972, thirty-two thousand; in 1973, thirty-five thousand. The beginning of this latter-day exodus, Solzhenitsyn concluded, "marked the end point of 200 years of Russians and Jews together. From then on, every Russian Jew enjoyed the possibility of deciding for himself: should he live in Russia or should he forsake the country. By the second half of the 1980s, emigration to Israel was already unproblematic."[84]

In his excellent *The Jewish Century*, Yuri Slezkine wrote this epitaph: "The Jewish part of Russian history is [now] over.... Most Jewish nationalist accounts of Soviet history have preserved the memory of Jewish victimization at the hands of the Whites, Nazis, Ukrainian nationalists, and the postwar Soviet state, but not the memory of the Jewish Revolution against Judaism, Jewish identification with Bolshevism, and the unparalleled Jewish success within the Soviet establishment of the 1920s and 1930s."[85]

Having reached the endpoint of two hundred years, Solzhenitsyn added a chapter on the question of Jewish assimilation. From the Napoleonic era on, he wrote, one country after another emancipated the Jews, the most educated of whom came to believe that they did not constitute a nation but were simply Poles, Germans, Frenchmen of the Mosaic faith. "Marx, and later Lenin, saw the solution to the Jewish question in a *complete* assimilation of Jews in the countries in which they lived."[86] Zionism, the Shoah, and the founding of the state of Israel led many Jews to reject that solution.

Solzhenitsyn believed that they were right to do so. "The key to the problem lies not in a fatal origin, not in blood, not in the genes, but in this question: *Whose* suffering lies nearer to one's heart: Jewish or the suffering of the core nation in the midst of which one came of age?" He had already formed his own answer. "All who have proposed the path of *universal* assimilation must sooner or later declare bankruptcy." He quickly added, however: "But there are nevertheless individuals who stand out, individual cases of assimilation in the fullest sense. And we in Russia bid such men and women welcome from the bottom of our hearts."[87]

In the late 1990s, as he was writing *Two Hundred Years Together*, Solzhenitsyn also penned a series of *Miniatures*, brief reflections, pensive and melancholic, that testify to his love of life and his calmness of spirit as he approached death. It was not the first time that he had found peace in this form of writing, so different from his magisterial and disquieting novels and histories. Between 1958 and 1960, he wrote seventeen miniatures—adding one more in 1963. Living abroad, he had found it impossible to write more because he needed the inspiration of Russia's nature and Russian life. Once returned to his native soil, he could again turn his everyday experiences into universal insights.

In one of the most moving of his miniatures, "Growing Old," Solzhenitsyn wrote that "aging is in no sense a punishment from on high, but brings its own blessings and a warmth of colors all its own." Knowing that his life was nearing its end, he obtained greater joy from life's small pleasures—the songs of birds, the beauties of nature—than ever before. He concluded with these wise words: "Growing old serenely is not a downhill path, but an ascent." His own serenity was broken only by the shame he felt as a result of the time of troubles into which his post-communist Motherland had fallen. "It oppresses you constantly, dogs your every step." In "A Prayer for Russia," therefore, he asked God "out of the depths of Calamity" to "Save your disordered people."[88]

WARNING TO THE WEST

According to Juliana Schmemann, Fr. Alexander Schmemann's *matushka* (wife), Solzhenitsyn's principal interests were writing, Holy Russia, and anti-Western thought.[1] Having been born to write and having lost long years in the GULag, he wrote as a man possessed in the years remaining to him; and as we know, the result was an œuvre of astonishing volume. Harassment by the KGB and hounding by the Western press made it difficult for him to preserve the peace and quiet he needed for work, but he allowed nothing to deter him, not least because he was on a mission to serve Holy (Orthodox) Russia.

To anti-Western thought (combined with a warning) he made an important contribution of his own. In the second volume of *Two Hundred Years Together*, for example, he took critical aim at Western intellectuals. Their enthusiasm for the Soviet Union's "social experiment" was, for a former *zek*, unfathomable—and so was their inability to make distinctions. "Fifteen million peasants were annihilated in the struggle against 'kulaks'; six million peasants starved to death in 1932; millions perished as a result of mass shootings and GULag terror"—and Western *bien-pensants* remained silent. Only when the Soviets denied Jews exit visas did they form committees, sign petitions, and march in protest through the streets of Manhattan.[2]

From long years in the United States, Solzhenitsyn had become convinced that most Western intellectuals sympathized with socialism, which, he pointed out, "uses the neat device of declaring all serious criticism 'outside the framework of possible discussion.'" By the time he returned home he had concluded that his warnings to the West about socialism's dangers, about atheism, and about cultural decadence were of little avail. In his Nobel lecture, he had pointed out that "countries and entire continents continually repeat each other's mistakes with a time lag . . . when, it would seem, everything is so very clear. But no: What one people has already endured, appraised and rejected suddenly emerges among another people as the very latest word."[3]

In the speech he delivered over the BBC radio network in March 1976, Solzhenitsyn identified some telltale similarities between prerevolutionary Russia and the contemporary West: "Adults deferring to the opinion of their children; the younger generation carried away by shallow, worthless ideas; professors scared of being unfashionable; journalists refusing to take responsibility for the words they squander so easily." For the Western press, Solzhenitsyn reserved a special contempt. Much to his initial surprise, he discovered that it differed little from the communist press in Russia. Journalists were as one in their preferences and their accepted patterns of judgment, and they transmitted to readers only those opinions that did not too openly contradict their own.[4]

Solzhenitsyn's most controversial indictment of Western decline, as we have seen, was the speech he delivered at Harvard in 1978,[5] prefaced by his assurance that he spoke "as a friend, not as an adversary." He was struck, he told an unsympathetic audience, by the fact that in the West "voluntary self-restraint is almost unheard of." He had heard much talk of "human rights" but little of human obligations. That state of affairs, he argued, could be traced back to the rationalistic humanism of the Enlightenment. "The humanistic way of thinking did not admit the existence of intrinsic evil in man, nor did it see any task higher than the attainment of happiness on earth." No wonder, then, that humanism merged with socialism. Solzhenitsyn put it this way: "As humanism in its development was becoming more and more materialistic, it also increasingly allowed its concepts to be used first by socialism and then by communism. So that Karl Marx was able to say, in 1844, that 'communism is naturalized humanism.'"

"This statement," he continued, "has proved to be not entirely unreasonable. One does see the same stones in the foundations of an eroded humanism and of any type of socialism: boundless materialism; freedom from religion and religious responsibility (which under Communist regimes attains the stage of antireligious dictatorship); concentration on social structures with an allegedly scientific approach."[6]

Just as thought was controlled in the Soviet Union, so was it in the West. Without any censorship, "fashionable trends of thought and ideas are fastidiously separated from those that are not fashionable, and the latter, without ever being forbidden, have little chance of finding their way into periodicals or books or being heard in colleges. Scholars are free in the legal sense, but they are hemmed in by the idols of the prevailing fad."[7]

Most Western commentators, we know, dismissed Solzhenitsyn's critique of the West as that of a Russian religious fanatic incapable of appreciating the virtues of secularism and democracy. To be sure, not everyone joined the chorus of indignation. Two years before Solzhenitsyn delivered his Harvard address, *Die Zeit* of Hamburg published a letter from George Kennan in which the distinguished diplomat and historian wrote of a West "succumbing feebly, day by day, to its own decadence, sliding into debility on the slime of its own self-indulgent permissiveness; its drugs, its crime, its pornography, its pampering of the youth, its addiction to its bodily comforts, its rampant materialism and consumerism."[8] As a student of Russian history, Kennan knew that Solzhenitsyn was right that the West was traveling a road similar to that which ended in the ruin of his own country.

Western societies, according to Solzhenitsyn, were "losing more and more of their religious essence as they thoughtlessly yield up their young generation to atheism."[9] And not the young generation alone. US courts, including the Supreme Court, declare most displays of the Decalogue to be "unconstitutional"—in fact, they hold that *any* sign of Christianity in the public square violates the Constitution. In Europe a reference to Christianity as an important part of European identity in the Preamble to the EU Constitutional Treaty had to be dropped because it was "incongruent with European values."

At about the time of Solzhenitsyn's death, popularizing "New Atheists"—men such as Richard Dawkins, Sam Harris, Daniel Dennett, and Christopher Hitchens—gained a large audience, even if, as the Orthodox philosopher/theologian David Bentley Hart pointed out, they lacked the seriousness and intelligence of Friedrich Nietzsche, the great German thinker who issued a challenge to the Christian faith difficult to ignore. "Today's gadflies seem far lazier, less insightful, less subtle, less refined, more emotional, more ethically complacent, and far more interested in facile simplifications of history than in sober and demanding investigations of what Christianity has been or is."[10]

On his list of similarities between prerevolutionary Russia and the contemporary West, Solzhenitsyn instanced the deference that Western adults show to the opinions of their children. In America, essayist Joseph Epstein writes, "we are currently living in a Kindergarchy, under rule by children." That means that "all arrangements are centered on children: their schooling, their lessons, their predilections, their care and feeding and general high maintenance."[11] It also means that children's opinions are taken with the utmost seriousness—President Jimmy Carter, when faced with some matter relating to nuclear weapons, sought his daughter's wisdom. The end result of treating the young as sages is that they believe themselves to be just that. "Today's youth," Solzhenitsyn noted in his Nobel lecture, "enthusiastically mouth the discredited clichés of the Russian nineteenth century, thinking that they are uncovering something new."[12]

When reporting on revolutionary terrorists of the kind that helped bring tsarist Russia to its knees, Solzhenitsyn found that Western journalists are careful to avoid the word "terrorist"—they prefer "militant." "When a government earnestly undertakes to root out terrorism," Solzhenitsyn told his Harvard audience, "public opinion immediately accuses it of violating the terrorists' civil rights."[13] In prerevolutionary Russia, too, there was "if not a cult of terror, then a fierce defense of terrorists. People in good positions—intellectuals, professors, liberals—spent a great deal of effort, anger, and indignation in defending terrorists."[14] Nor were Russian intellectuals, professors, and liberals alone. Attorneys and judges also showed greater concern for terrorists' rights than for victims' justice. Solzhenitsyn anticipated a similar trend in the West.

As an exile in the West, Solzhenitsyn witnessed a society sinking into what he called the "abyss of human decadence." He instanced in that regard "intolerable music," by which he meant music that coarsens public taste. Motion pictures were, Solzhenitsyn charged in the Harvard address, almost as bad as popular music, filled as they were with vile language, crime, horror, and pornography. We recall his shock when, on returning home, he found a Russia plagued by pornography, which he believed to have been imported from the West.

With respect to the so-called sexual revolution in general, Solzhenitsyn almost certainly would have agreed with Aldous Huxley, who, in a foreword to *Brave New World*, wrote that "as political and economic freedom diminishes, sexual freedom tends compensatingly to increase. And the dictator ... will do well to encourage that freedom. In conjunction with the freedom to day-dream under the influence of dope and movies and the radio, it will help to reconcile his subjects to the servitude which is their fate." In the novel Huxley's characters regularly use the drug soma "which raised a quite impenetrable wall between the actual universe and their minds."[15] Solzhenitsyn was aware that drug use in the West, and particularly in the United States, had raised a similar wall.

Twelve years after delivering his Harvard address and four years before returning home, Solzhenitsyn published in *Komsomolskaya Pravda* the article "How to Revitalize Russia" (translated as *Rebuilding Russia: Reflections and*

Tentative Proposals). In it he went out of his way to remind readers of some of the West's admirable features—its civil liberties, respect for the individual, freedom of personal activity, high level of general welfare, and charitable movements. He suggested too that Russia had something to learn from the wisdom of the great figures of the Western tradition, thinkers such as Plato, Aristotle, and Tocqueville.

Nevertheless, his view of what he called the West's "self-indulgent and squalid" mass culture remained the same as it was in 1978, and he deplored what Russian friends told him about its growing influence in Russia. Nor had he changed his view on the eve of his return home, when he granted an interview to *Forbes*. "Russia," he told the magazine's interviewer, "is currently adopting many things from the West. Unfortunately, it is also adopting many of the worst things. All the filth! Pornography, drug addiction, organized crime, new types of swindles."[16]

In 1998, four years after returning home, Solzhenitsyn granted a series of interviews to Joseph Pearce. He told the English-born Catholic writer that he had become convinced that, over the last two centuries, Russia and the West had completed a vicious circle; the West was—not always consciously—following a path similar to that taken by nineteenth-century Russia. Then, after the fall of communism, Russia adopted as *its* model the contemporary West. As a result, his country had entered "a blind alley and had nowhere to go." Pearce asked if he thought the West was stuck in the same blind alley. Solzhenitsyn's reply revealed much about his view of the historical-spiritual destinies of Russia and the West in the first years of his repatriation.

> Over the last twelve years I have stopped viewing Russia as something very distinct from the West. Today when we say the West we are already referring to the West and to Russia. We could use the word "modernity" if we exclude Africa, and the Islamic world, and partially China. With the exception of those areas we should not use the words "the West" but the word "modernity." The modern world. And yes, then I would say that there are ills that are characteristic, that have plagued the West for a long time and now Russia has quickly adopted them also.[17]

In the years since Solzhenitsyn's death, the crisis of modernity has only deepened—especially in the West. However critical the Western media, and hence

Western public opinion, may be of twenty-first-century Russia, Solzhenitsyn's last years were distinguished by a cautious optimism with respect to his country's historical and spiritual future. We know that he expressed confidence in President Putin, and in a *Der Spiegel* interview of 2007 he also spoke well of (then) Metropolitan (later Patriarch) Kirill, whose grandfather had been a prisoner on Solovki and who supported Putin's reforms.

Nevertheless, Solzhenitsyn continued to pray that Russians as well as Westerners would heed the warning he gave in his Templeton lecture. "The free people of the West could reasonably have been expected to realize that they are beset by numerous freely nurtured falsehoods, and not to allow lies to be foisted upon them so easily. All attempts to find a way out of the plight of today's world are fruitless unless we redirect our consciousness, in repentance, to the Creator of all: Without this, no exit will be illumined, and we shall seek it in vain."[18]

NOTES

CHAPTER ONE

1. Aleksandr Solzhenitsyn, *Lenin in Zurich*, trans. H. T. Willetts (New York: Farrar, Straus and Giroux, 1976), 103.

2. Dmitri Volkogonov, *Lenin: A New Biography*, trans. and ed. Harold Shukman (New York: Free Press, 1994), 373.

3. Tom Stoppard, *Travesties* (New York: Grove Press, 1975), 86.

4. Cited in Nathaniel Davis, *A Long Walk to Church: A Contemporary History of Russian Orthodoxy* (Boulder, CO: Westview Press, 1995), 213.

5. Volkogonov, *Lenin*, 235.

6. Cited in Ágnes Gereben, "A bolsevik állam és az ortodox egyház: 1917–1920," *Valóság* 44, no. 3 (2001): 79.

7. Alexander N. Yakolev, *A Century of Violence in Soviet Russia*, trans. Anthony Austin (New Haven, CT: Yale University Press, 2002), 156.

8. Dmitry S. Likhachev, *Reflections on the Russian Soul: A Memoir*, trans. Bernard Adams, trans. and ed. A. R. Tulloch (Budapest: Central European University Press, 2000), 64.

9. Gereben, "A bolsevik állam és az ortodox egyház," 86–87.

10. Nicolas Werth, "A State against Its People: Violence, Repression, and Terror in the Soviet Union," in *The Black Book of Communism: Crimes, Terror, Repression*, by Stéphane Courtois et al., trans. Jonathan Murphy and Mark Kramer (Cambridge, MA: Harvard University Press, 1999), 123–24.

11. Cited in ibid., 123.

12. Richard Pipes, ed., *The Unknown Lenin: From the Secret Archive*, trans. Catherine A. Fitzpatrick (New Haven, CT: Yale University Press, 1998 [1996], 154.

13. Cited in Dimitry Pospielovsky, *The Russian Church under the Soviet Regime, 1917–1982*, (Crestwood, NY: St. Vladimir's Seminary Press, 1984), 1:82.

14. Nicolas Zernov, *The Russian Religious Renaissance of the Twentieth Century* (New York: Harper and Row, 1963), 152.

15. Nicolas Berdyaev in Berdyaev et al., *Landmarks: A Collection of Essays on the Russian Intelligentsia, 1909*, ed. Boris Shragin and Albert Todd, trans. Marian Schwartz (New York: Karz Howard, 1977), 20.

16. Simeon Frank in ibid., 179.

17. Cited in Zernov, *Russian Religious Renaissance*, 128.

18. See V. I. Lenin, "Concerning *Vekhi*," http://www.marxists.org/archive/lenin/works/1909/dec/13.htm.

19. Aleksandr Solzhenitsyn, *The GULag Archipelago 1918–1956: An Experiment in Literary Investigation, 1–2*, trans. Thomas P. Whitney (New York: Harper and Row, 1973, 1974), 130.

20. Lesley Chamberlain, *Lenin's Private War: The Voyage of the Philosophy Steamer and the Exile of the Intelligentsia* (New York: Picador, 2008 [2006]), 4.

21. Nicolas Berdyaev, "Spirits of the Russian Revolution," http://www.berdyaev.com/berdiaev/berd_lib/1918_299.html, 1918.

22. Nicolas Berdyaev, *The Origin of Russian Communism*, trans. R. M. French (Ann Arbor: University of Michigan Press, 1960 [1937]), 40.

23. Cited in Joseph Frank, *Dostoevsky: The Miraculous Years, 1865–1871* (Princeton, NJ: Princeton University Press, 1995), 420.

24. Victor Afanasiev, *Elder Barsanuphius of Optina* (Platina, CA: St. Herman of Alaska Brotherhood, 2000), 483.

25. Cited in Joseph Frank, *Dostoevsky: The Mantle of the Prophet, 1871–1881* (Princeton, NJ: Princeton University Press, 2002), 473.

26. Nikolai Chernyshevsky, *What Is to Be Done?*, trans. Michael R. Katz; ann. William G. Wagner (Ithaca, NY: Cornell University Press, 1989), 28.

27. Berdyaev, *Origin of Russian Communism*, 8.

28. Chernyshevsky, *What Is to Be Done?*, 293.

29. Cited in ibid., 32.

30. Cited in Tibor Szamuely, *The Russian Tradition* (London: Fontana Press, 1988 [1974]), 345.

31. Cited in ibid., 346; see also Sergei Nechaev [and Mikhail Bakunin], "Catechism of a Revolutionist," http://pages.uoregon.edu/kimball/Nqv.catechism.thm.htm.

32. Fyodor Dostoyevsky, *The Devils*, trans. David Magarshack (London: Penguin Books, 1971 [1953]), 421.

33. Ibid., 692.

34. Feodor M. Dostoevsky, "Pushkin," in *Russian Intellectual History: An Anthology*, ed. Marc Raeff (New York: Harcourt, Brace and World, 1966), 300.

35. Cited in Szamuely, *Russian Tradition*, 345.

36. Cited in Volkogonov, *Lenin*, 383.

37. Cited in Simon Sebag Montefiore, *Young Stalin* (New York: Vintage Books, 2008), 64.

38. Cited in ibid., 56, 295.

39. Werth, "State against Its People," 73.

40. Anne Applebaum, *GULag: A History* (New York: Anchor Books, 2004), 9.

41. Aleksandr Solzhenitsyn, *The GULag Archipelago 1918–1956: An Experiment in Literary Investigation, 3–4*. Trans. Thomas P. Whitney (New York: Harper and Row, 1974/1975), 19.

42. This story is told wonderfully well by Roy R. Robson in *Solovki: The Story of Russia Told through Its Most Remarkable Islands* (New Haven, CT: Yale University Press, 2004).

43. Solzhenitsyn, *GULag Archipelago, 3–4*, 43.

44. Likhachev, *Reflections*, 119–20.

45. Solzhenitsyn, *GULag Archipelago, 3–4*, 60.

46. Likhachev, *Reflections*, 112.

47. Dariusz Tolczyk, *See No Evil: Literary Cover-Ups and Discoveries of the Soviet Camp Experience* (New Haven, CT: Yale University Press, 1999), 142–43.

48. Cited in Applebaum, *GULag*, 43.

49. Solzhenitsyn, *GULag Archipelago, 3–4*, 670.

50.   Cited in Avril Pyman, *Pavel Florensky: A Quiet Genius: The Tragic and Extraordinary Life of Russia's Unknown da Vinci* (New York: Continuum, 2010), 165–66.

51.   Ibid., 180–81, 209.

52.   Solzhenitsyn, *GULag Archipelago*, 3–4, 130.

53.   Robert Conquest, *Kolyma: The Arctic Death Camps* (New York: Viking, 1978), 124.

54.   Varlam Shalamov, *Kolyma Tales*, trans. John Glad (London: Penguin Books, 1994), 350.

55.   Ibid., 414.

56.   Ibid., 282.

57.   Conquest, *Kolyma*, 228.

58.   Ibid., 230.

59.   Solzhenitsyn, *GULag Archipelago*, 3–4, 599.

60.   Shalamov, *Kolyma Tales*, 450.

61.   Solzhenitsyn, *GULag Archipelago*, 3–4, 200.

62.   Cited in Joseph Pearce, *Solzhenitsyn: A Soul in Exile* (Grand Rapids, MI: Baker Books, 2001 [1999]), 15.

63.   Cited in ibid., 32.

64.   Aleksandr Solzhenitsyn, "The Smatterers," in Solzhenitsyn et al., *From Under the Rubble*, trans. Michael Scammell et al. (New York: Bantam Books, 1976), 239.

65.   Martin Malia, *The Soviet Tragedy: A History of Socialism in Russia, 1917–1991* (New York: Free Press, 1994), 283.

66.   Cited in Pearce, *Solzhenitsyn*, 52.

67.   Solzhenitsyn, *GULag Archipelago*, 1–2, 162.

68.   Aleksandr Solzhenitsyn, *Apricot Jam and Other Stories*, trans. Kenneth Lantz and Stephan Solzhenitsyn (Berkeley: Counterpoint, 2011), 238.

69.   Ibid, 249.

70.   Antony Beevor in Vasily Grossman, *A Writer at War: A Soviet Journalist with the Red Army, 1941–1945*, ed. and trans. Antony Beevor and Luba Vinogradova (New York: Vintage Books, 2007), 155.

71.   Richard Overy, *Russia's War: A History of the Soviet War Effort: 1941–1945* (New York: Penguin Books, 1998), 183.

72.   Vasily Grossman, *Life and Fate*, trans. Robert Chandler (New York: New York Review Books, 2006), 664.

73.   J. Glenn Gray, *The Warriors: Reflections on Men in Battle.* (Lincoln: University of Nebraska Press, 1998 [1959]), 25.

74.   Solzhenitsyn, *Apricot Jam*, 189.

75.   Overy, *Russia's War*, 201.

76.   Solzhenitsyn, *GULag Archipelago*, 1–2, 256.

77.   Aleksandr Solzhenitsyn, *The GULag Archipelago, 1918–1956: An Experiment in Literary Investigation, 5–7*, trans. Harry Willetts (New York: Harper and Row, 1978), 99.

78.   Leszek Kolakowski, *Is God Happy? Selected Essays* (New York: Basic Books, 2013), 60.

79.   Cited in Simon Sebag Montefiore, *Stalin: The Court of the Red Tsar* (New York: Vintage Books, 2005 [2003]), 479.

80.   Solzhenitsyn, *GULag Archipelago*, 1–2, 21.

81.   Aleksandr Solzhenitsyn, *Prussian Nights: A Poem*, trans. Robert Conquest (New York: Farrar, Straus and Giroux, 1977), 103, 105.

82.   Edward E. Ericson and Alexis Klimoff, *The Soul and Barbed Wire: An Introduction to Solzhenitsyn* (Wilmington, DE: ISI Books, 2008), 72, 247n3.

Chapter Two

1.   Natalia Solzhenitsyn, "Returning to 'The GULag,'" trans. Alexis Klimoff, intro. Daniel J. Mahoney, *New Criterion* 31, no. 1 (2012): 5.

2.   Solzhenitsyn, *GULag Archipelago, 1–2*, 611–12.

3.   Dimitri Panin, *The Notebooks of Sologdin*, trans. John Moore (New York: Harcourt Brace Jovanovich, 1976), 43n.

4.   Solzhenitsyn, *GULag Archipelago, 1–2*, 563–64.

5.   Cited in Pearce, *Solzhenitsyn*, 91.

6.   Solzhenitsyn, *GULag Archipelago, 1–2*, 602.

7.   Aleksandr Solzhenitsyn, *In the First Circle: A Novel*, trans. Harry T. Willetts (New York: Harper/Perennial, 2009), 554.

8.   Panin, *Notebooks of Sologdin*, 263.

9.   Solzhenitsyn, *First Circle*, 178, 43.

10.   Ibid., 201, 179.

11.   Ibid., 144, 328.

12.   Cited in Paul Hollander, *The End of Commitment: Intellectuals, Revolutionaries, and Political Morality* (Chicago: Ivan R. Dee, 2006), 40–41.

13.   Ibid., 43.

14.   Panin, *Notebooks of Sologdin*, 259.

15.   Solzhenitsyn, *First Circle*, 339–40.

16.   Ibid., 441.

17.   Ibid., 447.

18.   Ibid., 495.

19.   Solzhenitsyn, *GULag Archipelago, 5–7*, 37.

20.   Solzhenitsyn, *GULag Archipelago, 3–4*, 610.

21.   Solzhenitsyn, *GULag Archipelago, 5–7*, 98.

22.   Aleksandr Solzhenitsyn, *One Day in the Life of Ivan Denisovich*, trans. H. T. Willetts (New York: Farrar, Straus and Giroux, 2005), 86.

23.   Ibid., 116.

24.   Ibid., 176–77.

25.   Solzhenitsyn, *GULag Archipelago, 3–4*, 613.

26.   Cited in ibid., 618.

27.   Ibid., 626.

28.   Ibid., 614–15.

29.   Ibid., 615.

30.   Solzhenitsyn, *GULag Archipelago, 5–7*, 421.

31.   Ibid., 428.

32.   Ibid., 440.

33.   Leo Tolstoy, "What Men Live By," in *Master and Man and Other Stories*, trans. Ronald Wilks and Paul Foote (London: Penguin Books, 2005), 166.

34.   Aleksandr Solzhenitsyn, *Cancer Ward*, trans. Nicholas Bethell and David Burg (New York: Farrar, Straus and Giroux, 1969), 119.

35. Ibid., 300.

36. Ibid., 441–42.

37. Ibid., 150.

38. Ibid., 290.

39. Ibid., 531, 273.

40. Ibid., 509, 536.

41. Aleksandr Solzhenitsyn, *The Love-Girl and the Innocent*, trans. Nicholas Bethell and David Burg (New York: Farrar, Straus and Giroux, 1969), 39, 48, 84.

42. Ibid., 85, 97.

43. Ibid., 22, 96.

44. Solzhenitsyn, *GULag Archipelago, 5–7*, 440.

CHAPTER THREE

1. Aleksandr Solzhenitsyn, "Matryona's Home," in *The Solzhenitsyn Reader: New and Essential Writings 1947–2005*, ed. Edward E. Ericson, Jr. and Daniel J. Mahoney (Wilmington, DE: ISI Books, 2006), 24–56.

2. Pearce, *Solzhenitsyn*, 142.

3. Cited in ibid., 148.

4. Cited in Natalia Solzhenitsyn, "Returning," 6.

5. Cited in Tolczyk, *See No Evil*, 281.

6. Michael Scammell, ed., *The Solzhenitsyn Files: Secret Soviet Documents Reveal One Man's Fight Against the Monolith*, trans. by Catherine A. Fitzpatrick et al. (Chicago: edition q, 1995), 5n.

7. Aleksandr Solzhenitsyn, *Invisible Allies*, trans. Alexis Klimoff and Michael Nicholson (Washington, DC: Counterpoint, 1995), 30.

8. Davis, *Long Walk to Church*, 34.

9. Cited in Michael Bourdeaux, *Patriarch and Prophets: Persecution of the Russian Orthodox Church Today* (New York: Praeger, 1970), 23.

10. Cited in ibid., 38.

11. William C. Fletcher, *The Russian Orthodox Church Underground, 1917–1970* (London: Oxford University Press, 1971), 255–56.

12. Nikita Struve, *Christians in Contemporary Russia*, trans. Lancelot Sheppard and A. Manson (New York: Charles Scribner's Sons, 1967), 297–98.

13. Pospielovsky, *Russian Church*, 2:343.

14. Aleksandr Solzhenitsyn, *The Oak and the Calf: Sketches of Literary Life in the Soviet Union*, trans. Harry Willetts (New York: Harper and Row, 1979), 90.

15. Scammell, *Solzhenitsyn Files*, 26–27.

16. Max Hayward, ed., *On Trial: The Soviet State versus "Abram Tertz" and "Nikolai Arzhak,"* trans. Max Hayward (New York: Harper and Row, 1967), 37–38.

17. Abram Tertz (Andrei Sinyavsky), *On Socialist Realism*, trans. George Dennis (New York: Pantheon Books, 1960), 57.

18. Ibid., 60, 66.

19. Hayward, *On Trial*, 90–91.

20. Nikolai Arzhak (Yuli Daniel), "Hands: A Story," *Dissent* 13, no. 4 (1966), 391–95.

21. Hayward, *On Trial*, 65, 68.

22. Ibid., 30.

23. Ibid., 290, 287.

24. Solzhenitsyn, *Invisible Allies*, 113, 130.

25. Struve, *Christians in Contemporary Russia*, 404–17.

26. Bourdeaux, *Patriarch and Prophets*, 194–221.

27. Ibid., 218.

28. Ibid., 224, 226–27.

29. Solzhenitsyn, *Oak and Calf*, 150–51.

30. Aleksandr Solzhenitsyn, "Lenten Letter to Patriarch Pimen of Russia," in John B. Dunlop et al., eds., *Aleksandr Solzhenitsyn: Critical Essays and Documentary Materials*, 2nd ed. (New York: Collier Books, 1975), 550–55.

31. "The Easter Procession," in Solzhenitsyn, *Solzhenitsyn Reader*, 57–61.

32. Vladislav Zubok, *Zhivago's Children: The Last Russian Intelligentsia* (Cambridge, MA: Belknap Press of Harvard University Press, 2009), 252–53.

33. Solzhenitsyn, *Invisible Allies*, 214.

34. Ibid., 213–14.

35. *Scammell, Solzhenitsyn Files*, 9.

36. Solzhenitsyn, *Oak and Calf*, 458–62.

37. George F. Kennan, "Between Earth and Hell," in Dunlop et al., *Aleksandr Solzhenitsyn*, 505.

38. Solzhenitsyn, *GULag Archipelago*, 1–2, 160–61.

39. Ibid., 168.

40. Ibid., 223.

41. Solzhenitsyn, *GULag Archipelago*, 3–4, 200–201.

42. Ibid., 204, 540.

43. Solzhenitsyn, *GULag Archipelago*, 5–7, 80.

44. Solzhenitsyn, *GULag Archipelago*, 3–4, 641.

45. Applebaum, *GULag*, 20.

46. Solzhenitsyn, *GULag Archipelago*, 1–2, 549.

47. Solzhenitsyn, *GULag Archipelago*, 3–4, 85.

48. Ibid., 578, 586.

49. Solzhenitsyn, *GULag Archipelago*, 5–7, 93, 97.

50. Ibid., 235.

51. Ibid., 259.

52. Ibid., 290.

53. Ibid., 324, 326.

54. Solzhenitsyn, *Oak and Calf*, 536.

55. Solzhenitsyn, *Invisible Allies*, 127.

56. Solzhenitsyn, *Oak and Calf*, 249.

57. Solzhenitsyn, *Invisible Allies*, 111.

58. Andrei D. Sakharov, *Sakharov Speaks* (New York: Vintage Books, 1974), 55–114.

59. Thomas, *Alexander Solzhenitsyn*, 338.

60. Cited by Harrison E. Salisbury in Sakharov, *Sakharov Speaks*, 23.

61. Michael Scammell, *Solzhenitsyn: A Biography* (New York: W. W. Norton, 1984), 659–60.

62. Natalya A. Reshetovskaya, *Sanya: My Life with Aleksandr Solzhenitsyn*, trans. Elena Ivanoff (Indianapolis: Bobbs-Merrill, 1975), 112.

63. Solzhenitsyn, *Invisible Allies*, 198, 201.

64. Solzhenitsyn, *Oak and Calf*, 270.

65. Elizabeth Wilson, *Rostropovich: The Musical Life of the Great Cellist, Teacher, and Legend* (Chicago: Ivan R. Dee, 2008), 337.

66. Pyotr Struve in Berdyaev, et al., *Landmarks*, 148.

67. Interview with Matushka Juliana Schmemann, conducted by Carol Congdon and Cynthia Patzig, 2010.

68. Solzhenitsyn, *Invisible Allies*, 223, 250.

69. Aleksandr Solzhenitsyn, *Letter to the Soviet Leaders*, trans. Hilary Sternberg (New York: Harper and Row in association with Index on Censorship, 1974), 44n.

70. Sergei Bulgakov, *Karl Marx as a Religious Type: His Relation to the Religion of Anthropotheism of L. Feuerbach*, trans. Luba Barna, ed. Virgil R. Lang (Belmont, MA: Nordland Publishing Company, 1979 [1907]), 61.

71. Sergei Bulgakov, "Heroism and Asceticism: Reflections on the Religious Nature of the Russian Intelligentsia," in Berdyaev et al., *Landmarks*, 29, 44.

72. Solzhenitsyn, "The Smatterers," in Solzhenitsyn et al., *From Under the Rubble*, 229, 271.

73. Ibid, 234.

74. Alexander Solzhenitsyn, "As Breathing and Consciousness Return," in Solzhenitsyn et al., *From Under the Rubble*, 22–23.

75. Ibid., 20.

76. Edmund Burke, *Reflections on the Revolution in France*, ed. Conor Cruise O'Brien (New York: Penguin Books, 1968 [1790]), 91.

77. Ibid., 228.

78. Solzhenitsyn, "As Breathing and Consciousness Return," 21.

79. Ibid., 22.

80. Malia, *The Soviet Tragedy*, 498.

81. Solzhenitsyn, "As Breathing and Consciousness Return," 10.

82. Alexander Solzhenitsyn, "Repentance and Self-Limitation in the Life of Nations," in Solzhenitsyn et al., *From Under the Rubble*, 128.

83. Ibid., 112.

84. Solzhenitsyn, "Repentance and Self-Limitation in the Life of Nations," 134, 136.

85. Solzhenitsyn, *Oak and Calf*, 406.

86. Igor Shafarevich, *The Socialist Phenomenon*, trans. William Tjalsma, foreword Aleksandr I. Solzhenitsyn, 78. http://robertlstephens.com/essays/shafarevich/001SocialistPhenomenon.html.

87. Igor Shafarevich, "Socialism in Our Past and Future," in Solzhenitsyn et al., *From Under The Rubble*, 35.

88. Cited in Shafarevich, *The Socialist Phenomenon*, 107.

89. Cited in Shafarevich, "Socialism in Our Past and Future," 52; see also, Dostoevsky, *The Devils*, 418–19.

90. *Scammell, Solzhenitsyn Files, 142–43.*

91. Ibid., 197.

92. Solzhenitsyn, *Letter to the Soviet Leaders*, 17.

93.   Ibid., 52–53, 57.

94.   *Scammell, Solzhenitsyn Files,* 257.

95.   Ibid., 291.

CHAPTER FOUR

1.   Alexandre Soljénitsyne, *Le grain tombé entre les meules: Esquisses d'exil. Première partie, 1974–1978,* trans. Geneviève et José Johannet (Paris: Fayard, 1998), 11.

2.   Cited in Scammell, *Solzhenitsyn,* 948.

3.   Soljénitsyne, *Le grain tombé,* 165.

4.   Ibid., 58, 298.

5.   Aleksandr Solzhenitsyn, "Letter to the Third Council of the Russian Church Abroad," in Niels C. Nielsen, Jr., *Solzhenitsyn's Religion* (Nashville: Thomas Nelson, 1975), 156.

6.   James W. Cunningham, *A Vanquished Hope: The Movement for Church Renewal in Russia, 1905–1906* (Crestwood, NY: St. Vladimir's Seminary Press, 1981), 34.

7.   Roy R. Robson, *Old Believers in Modern Russia* (DeKalb: Northern Illinois University Press, 1995), 16.

8.   Cunningham, *A Vanquished Hope,* 35.

9.   Solzhenitsyn, "Letter," in Nielsen, *Solzhenitsyn's Religion,* 153.

10.   Robson, *Old Believers,* 23.

11.   Thomas, *Alexander Solzhenitsyn,* 450.

12.   Alexander Solzhenitsyn, *Warning to the West,* trans. Harris L. Coulter and Nataly Martin, ed. Alexis Klimoff (New York: Farrar, Straus and Giroux, 1976), 53.

13.   Ibid., 123, 136.

14.   Ibid., 136.

15.   Ibid., 144.

16.   Cited in Thomas, *Alexander Solzhenitsyn,* 455.

17.   Juliana Schmemann, *My Journey with Father Alexander* (Montréal: Alexander Press, 2006), 85; interview with Matushka Juliana Schmemann.

18.   Aleksandr I. Solzhenitsyn in Ronald Berman, ed., *Solzhenitsyn at Harvard* (Washington, DC: Ethics and Public Policy Center, 1980), 12.

19.   Ibid., 19.

20.   Soljénitsyne, *Le grain tombé entre les meules,* 420.

21.   Berman, ed., *Solzhenitsyn at Harvard,* 26, 60, 27, 42.

22.   Ibid., 28.

23.   Ibid., 23, 33.

24.   Ibid., 120–21.

25.   Richard Pipes, *Vixi: Memoirs of a Non-Belonger* (New Haven, CT: Yale University Press, 2003), 114–15.

26.   Berman, ed., *Solzhenitsyn at Harvard,* 94, 86.

27.   Ibid., 78.

28.   Pearce, *Solzhenitsyn,* 242.

29.   Cited by Nikita Struve in Alexander Schmemann, *I Believe . . . : Celebration of Faith,* I (Crestwood, NY: St. Vladimir's Seminary Press, 2003), 7.

30.   Alexander Schmemann, *I Believe,* 80.

31.   Alexander Schmemann, "On Solzhenitsyn," in Dunlop et al., eds., *Aleksandr Solzhenitsyn,* 39, 42.

32. Aleksandr Solzhenitsyn in Dunlop et al., eds., *Aleksandr Solzhenitsyn*, 44.

33. Alexander Schmemann, *The Journals of Father Alexander Schmemann 1973–1983*, trans. Juliana Schmemann (Crestwood, NY: St. Vladimir's Seminary Press, 2002), 38.

34. Soljénitsyne, *Le grain tombé entre les meules*, 139.

35. Interview with Matushka Juliana Schmemann.

36. Schmemann, *The Journals*, 43.

37. Ibid., 61.

38. Telephone interview with Fr. Andrew Tregubov, who knew both men well. July 5, 2014.

39. Alexander Schmemann, *The Historical Road of Eastern Orthodoxy*, trans. Lydia W. Kesich (Crestwood, NY: St. Vladimir's Seminary Press, 2003), 338.

40. Telephone interview with Fr. Andrew Tregubov.

41. Schmemann, *The Journals*, 32.

42. Ibid., 67, 74–75.

43. Ibid., 76–77.

44. Ibid., 315, 262.

45. See Solzhenitsyn, *Solzhenitsyn Reader*, 576–84.

46. Solzhenitsyn, *Warning to the West*, 112.

47. Henry Ashby Turner, Jr., *Hitler's Thirty Days to Power: January 1933* (Reading, MA: Addison-Wooley, 1996), 166.

48. Ibid., 176, 183.

49. Aleksandr Solzhenitsyn, *August 1914: The Red Wheel/Knot I*, trans. H. T Willetts (New York: Noonday/Farrar, Straus and Giroux, 1989), 324.

50. Ibid., 307.

51. Ibid., 107.

52. Ibid., 467.

53. Ibid., 451.

54. Ibid., 455–56.

55. See Lee Congdon, "Lukács, Camus, and the Russian Terrorists," *Continuity*, no. 1 (1980), 17–36.

56. Cited in ibid., 18.

57. Solzhenitsyn, *August 1914*, 346.

58. Ibid., 470, 575.

59. Ibid., 546.

60. Cited in Vladimir Danilenko, "The Assassination of Pyotr Stolypin, 1911: A Collection of Documents." www.eastview.com/files/StolypinEngReview.pdf.

61. Solzhenitsyn, *August 1914*, 537.

62. Ibid., 566.

63. Ibid., 568.

64. Ibid., 653.

65. Ibid., 470.

66. Abraham Ascher, *P.A. Stolypin: The Search for Stability in Late Imperial Russia* (Stanford: Stanford University Press, 2001), 378.

67. Solzhenitsyn, *August 1914*, 636

68. Aleksandr Solzhenitsyn, *November 1916: The Red Wheel/Knot II*, trans. H. T. Willetts (New York: Farrar, Straus and Giroux, 1999), 120.

69. Ibid., 74, 976.

70. Ibid., 76.

71. Ibid., 65–69.
72. Ibid., 541.
73. Ibid., 558.
74. Ibid., 562–63.
75. Ibid., 684.
76. Ibid., 907.
77. Ibid., 829.
78. Malia, *The Soviet Tragedy*, 143.
79. Solzhenitsyn, *November 1916*, 815.
80. Cited in Lincoln, *Red Victory*, 486.
81. Solzhenitsyn, *November 1916*, 984.
82. Ibid., 191.
83. Ibid., 988, 991.
84. Ibid., 993, 997, 1000.
85. Solzhenitsyn, *Solzhenitsyn Reader*, 400.
86. Ibid., 416.
87. Ibid., 408.
88. Ibid., 430.
89. Ibid., 454.
90. Ibid., 455.
91. Ibid., 463.
92. Aleksandr Solzhenitsyn, *Rebuilding Russia: Reflections and Tentative Proposals*, trans. Alexis Klimoff (New York: Farrar, Straus and Giroux, 1991), 47.
93. Ibid., 49.
94. Ibid., 62.
95. Ibid., 66.
96. Ibid., 97.
97. Lee Congdon, *George Kennan: A Writing Life* (Wilmington, DE: ISI Books, 2008), 121.
98. Solzhenitsyn, *Solzhenitsyn Reader*, 591–601.
99. Ibid., 602–605.

Chapter Five

1. Solzhenitsyn, *Solzhenitsyn Reader*, 609.
2. Thomas, *Alexander Solzhenitsyn*, 503.
3. "*Spiegel* Interview with Alexander Solzhenitsyn: 'I Am Not Afraid of Death.'" http://www.spiegel.de/international/world/Spiegel-interview-with-alexander-solzhenitsyn.
4. Solzhenitsyn, *Solzhenitsyn Reader*, 464–84.
5. Both cited in Daniel Treisman, *The Return: Russia's Journey from Gorbachev to Medvedev* (New York: Free Press, 2011), 90, 114.
6. Ibid., 93.
7. Paul Robinson, "Putin's Philosophy," *The American Conservative*, http://www.theamericanconservative.com/blog/putins-philosophy.
8. Vladimir Putin, *First Person: An Astonishingly Frank Self-Portrait*, trans. Catherine A. Fitzpatrick. With Nataliya Gevorkyan, Natalya Timakova, and Andrei Kolesnikov (New York: Public Affairs, 2000), 141–42.

9. *Spiegel* Interview with Alexander Solzhenitsyn."

10. Allen C. Lynch, *Vladimir Putin and Russian Statecraft* (Washington, DC: Potomac Books, 2011), 13.

11. Davis, *Long Walk to Church*, 217.

12. John and Carol Garrard, *Russian Orthodoxy Resurgent: Faith and Power in the New Russia* (Princeton: Princeton University Press, 2008), 242–43.

13. Ibid., 201.

14. Cited in Thomas, *Alexander Solzhenitsyn*, 494.

15. Cited in F. Roger Devlin, "Solzhenitsyn on the Jews and Tsarist Russia." http://toqonline.com/archives/v8n3/TOQv8n3Devlin.pdf.

16. Solzhenitsyn, *Solzhenitsyn Reader*, 489.

17. Aleksandr Solzhenitsyn, *"Zweihundert Jahre zusammen,"* vol. 1: *Die russisch-jüdische Geschichte 1795–1916*, trans. Kurt Baudisch und Holger von Rauch (Munich: Herbig, 2002 [2001], 240.

18. Ibid., 181, 184, 201.

19. Ibid., 310.

20. Ibid., 311.

21. Ibid., 321.

22. Solzhenitsyn, *Solzhenitsyn Reader*, 496.

23. Solzhenitsyn, *"Zweihundert Jahre,"* 1:135.

24. See W. Bruce Lincoln, *The Great Reforms: Autocracy, Bureaucracy, and the Politics of Change in Imperial Russia* (DeKalb: Northern Illinois University Press, 1990).

25. Solzhenitsyn, *"Zweihundert Jahre,"* 1:163, 174.

26. Ibid., 180.

27. Ibid., 184.

28. Ibid., 201, 196.

29. Ibid., 262.

30. Ibid., 266.

31. Solzhenitsyn, *Solzhenitsyn Reader*, 491–92.

32. Solzhenitsyn, *"Zweihundert Jahre,"* 1:276.

33. Solzhenitsyn, *Solzhenitsyn Reader*, 496.

34. Solzhenitsyn, *"Zweihundert Jahre,"* 1:166.

35. Ibid., 172.

36. Ibid., 236.

37. Ibid., 242.

38. Ibid., 241.

39. Ibid., 257.

40. Ibid., 248.

41. Ibid., 254.

42. Ibid., 346.

43. Ibid., 409, 419.

44. Solzhenitsyn, *Solzhenitsyn Reader*, 493–94, 496.

45. Solzhenitsyn, *"Zweihundert Jahre,"* 1:460.

46. Ibid., 461–62.

47. Ibid., 466.

48. Aleksandr Solzhenitsyn, *"Zweihundert Jahre zusammen,"* vol. 2: *Die Juden in der Sowjetunion*, trans. Andrea Wöhr and Peter Nordquist (Munich: Herbig, 2003 [2002]), 490.

49. Ibid., 40.

50. Ibid., 90–92.

51. Solzhenitsyn, *Solzhenitsyn Reader*, 498–99, 505.

52. Volkogonov, *Lenin*, 211.

53. Solzhenitsyn, *"Zweihundert Jahre zusammen,"* 2:137.

54. Cited in Yuri Slezkine, *The Jewish Century* (Princeton, NJ: Princeton University Press, 2004), 177.

55. Solzhenitsyn, *"Zweihundert Jahre zusammen,"* 2:109.

56. Ibid., 118.

57. Solzhenitsyn, *Solzhenitsyn Reader*, 506.

58. W. Bruce Lincoln, *Red Victory: A History of the Russian Civil War*, (New York: Simon and Schuster, 1989), 322–23.

59. Solzhenitsyn, *"Zweihundert Jahre zusammen,"* 2:335, 339.

60. Slezkine, *Jewish Century*, 236.

61. Ibid., 254–55.

62. Solzhenitsyn, *"Zweihundert Jahre zusammen,"* 2:303, 309.

63. Ibid., 305, 308.

64. Ibid., 323.

65. Ibid., 373.

66. Grossman, *Writer at War*, 249–50.

67. Antony Beevor in ibid., 250.

68. Solzhenitsyn, *"Zweihundert Jahre zusammen,"* 2:393.

69. Ibid., 399–400.

70. Ibid., 401–402.

71. Ibid., 403.

72. Solzhenitsyn, *GULag Archipelago, 3–4*, 612.

73. Ibid., 613.

74. Solzhenitsyn, *"Zweihundert Jahre zusammen,"* 2:410.

75. Montefiore, *Stalin*, 573–74.

76. Robert Conquest, *The Great Terror: A Reassessment* (New York: Oxford University Press, 1990), 122.

77. Solzhenitsyn, *"Zweihundert Jahre zusammen,"* 2:429.

78. Ibid., 442.

79. Ibid.

80. Ibid., 444.

81. Cited in Slezkine, *Jewish Century*, 353.

82. Solzhenitsyn, *"Zweihundert Jahre zusammen,"* 2:447.

83. Ibid., 489.

84. Ibid., 506, 514.

85. Slezkine, *Jewish Century*, 360.

86. Solzhenitsyn, *"Zweihundert Jahre zusammen,"* 2:519.

87. Ibid., 534–35.

88. Solzhenitsyn, *Solzhenitsyn Reader*, 629–30, 634.

CHAPTER SIX

1. Interview with Matushka Juliana Schmemann, conducted by Carol Congdon and Cynthia Patzig.

2. Solzhenitsyn, *"Zweihundert Jahre zusammen,"* 2:503–504.

3. Solzhenitsyn, *Solzhenitsyn Reader*, 519.

4. Aleksandr Solzhenitsyn, *Warning to the West*, trans. Harris L. Coulter and Nataly Martin, ed. Alexis Klimoff (New York: Farrar, Straus and Giroux), 53, 130.

5. Ronald Berman, ed., *Solzhenitsyn at Harvard*, (Washington, DC: Ethics and Public Policy Center, 1980), 3–20.

6. Ibid., 17–18

7. Ibid., 11.

8. George Kennan in Martin F. Herz, ed., *Decline of the West? George Kennan and His Critics* (Washington, DC: Ethics and Public Policy Center, 1978), 8.

9. Solzhenitsyn, *Solzhenitsyn Reader*, 581.

10. David Bentley Hart, *Atheist Delusions: The Christian Revolution and Its Fashionable Enemies* (New Haven: Yale University Press, 2009), 6.

11. Joseph Epstein, *A Literary Education and Other Essays* (Edinburg, VA: Axios Press, 2014), 121, 127.

12. Solzhenitsyn, *Solzhenitsyn Reader*, 522.

13. Berman, *Solzhenitsyn at Harvard*, 9.

14. Solzhenitsyn, *Warning*, 103.

15. Aldous Huxley, *Brave New World* (New York: Harper and Row/Perennial Library, 1969 [1932, 1946]), xviii, 78.

16. "Alexander Solzhenitsyn on The New Russia," http://www.forbes.com/2008/08/05/solzhenitsyn-forbes-interview-oped-cx_pm_0804russia.

17. "An Interview with Alexander Solzhenitsyn," conducted by Joseph Pearce. *St. Austin Review* 2, no. 2 (2003).

18. Solzhenitsyn, *Solzhenitsyn Reader*, 583.

BIBLIOGRAPHY

UNPUBLISHED SOURCES

Interviews

Matushka Juliana Schmemann (Mrs. Alexander; conducted by Carol Congdon and Cynthia
    Patzig)—December 2010; April 2013
Fr. Andrew Tregubov (telephone)—July 5, 2014

PUBLISHED SOURCES

Books by Aleksandr Solzhenitsyn

Apricot Jam and Other Stories. Translated by Kenneth Lantz and Stephan Solzhenitsyn.
    Berkeley: Counterpoint, 2011.
August 1914: The Red Wheel/Knot I. Translated by H. T. Willetts. New York: Noonday/
    Farrar, Straus and Giroux, 1989.
Cancer Ward. Translated by Nicholas Bethell and David Burg. New York: Farrar, Straus,
    and Giroux, 1969.
From Under the Rubble (with others). Translated by Michael Scammell et al. New York:
    Bantam Books, 1976.
Le grain tombé entre les meules: Esquisses d'exil. Première partie, 1974–1978. Translated by
    Geneviève and José Johannet. Paris: Fayard, 1998.
The GULag Archipelago, 1918–1956: An Experiment in Literary Investigation, 1–2. Trans-
    lated by Thomas P. Whitney. New York: Harper and Row, 1973.
The GULag Archipelago, 1918–1956: An Experiment in Literary Investigation, 3–4. Translated
    by Thomas P. Whitney. New York: Harper and Row, 1974/1975.
The GULag Archipelago, 1918–1956: An Experiment in Literary Investigation, 5–7. Translated
    by Harry Willetts. New York: Harper and Row, 1978.
In the First Circle: A Novel. Translated by Harry T. Willetts. New York: Harper/Perennial,
    2009.
Invisible Allies. Translated by Alexis Klimoff and Michael Nicholson. Washington, DC:
    Counterpoint, 1995.
Lenin in Zurich. Translated by H. T. Willetts. New York: Farrar, Straus and Giroux, 1976.
Letter to the Soviet Leaders. Translated by Hilary Sternberg. New York: Harper and Row (in
    association with Index on Censorship), 1974.
The Love-Girl and the Innocent. Translated by Nicholas Bethell and David Burg. New York:
    Farrar, Straus and Giroux, 1969.
November 1916: The Red Wheel/Knot II. Translated by H. T. Willetts. New York: Farrar,
    Straus and Giroux, 1999.

The Oak and the Calf: Sketches of Literary Life in the Soviet Union. Translated by Harry Willetts. New York: Harper and Row, 1979.

One Day in the Life of Ivan Denisovich. Translated by H. T. Willetts. New York: Farrar, Straus and Giroux, 2005.

A Pictorial Autobiography. New York: Farrar, Straus and Giroux, 1974.

Prussian Nights: A Poem. Translated by Robert Conquest. New York: Farrar, Straus and Giroux, 1977.

Rebuilding Russia: Reflections and Tentative Proposals. Translated by Alexis Klimoff. New York: Farrar, Straus and Giroux, 1991.

"The Russian Question" at the End of the Twentieth Century. Translated by Yermolai Solzhenitsyn. New York: Farrar, Straus and Giroux, 1995.

The Solzhenitsyn Reader: New and Essential Writings, 1947–2005. Edited by Edward E. Ericson, Jr. and Daniel J. Mahoney. Wilmington, DE: ISI Books, 2006.

The Voice of Freedom. Washington, DC: AFL and CIO, n.d. [1975].

Voices from the GULag (editor). Translated by Kenneth Lantz. Evanston: Northwestern University Press, 2010.

Warning to the West. Translated by Harris L. Coulter and Nataly Martin. Edited by Alexis Klimoff. New York: Farrar, Straus and Giroux, 1976.

"Zweihundert Jahre zusammen." Vol. 1: *Die russisch-jüdische Geschichte, 1795–1916.* Translated by Kurt Baudisch and Holger von Rauch. Munich: Herbig, 2002 [2001]. Vol. 2: *Die Juden in der Sowjetunion.* Translated by Andrea Wöhr and Peter Nordquist. Munich: Herbig, 2003 [2002].

Interviews with Aleksandr Solzhenitsyn

"Alexander Solzhenitsyn on the New Russia." http://www.forbes.com/2008/08/05/solzhenitsyn-forbes-interview-oped-cx_pm_0804russia.

"An Interview with Alexander Solzhenitsyn." Conducted by Joseph Pearce. *St. Austin Review* 2, no. 2 (2003).

"Interview with Solzhenitsyn about '200 Years Together.'" Conducted by Lydia Chukovskaya. http://www.orthodoxytoday.org/articles/ChukovskayaSolzhenitsyn.php.

"Solzhenitsyn in Zurich: An Interview." *Encounter*, April 1976, 9–14.

"*Spiegel* Interview with Alexander Solzhenitsyn: 'I Am Not Afraid of Death.'" http://www.spiegel.de/international/world/spiegel-interview-with-alexander-solzhenitsyn.

OTHER PRIMARY SOURCES

Arzhak, Nikolai (Yuli Daniel). "Hands: A Story." *Dissent* 13, no. 4 (1966): 391–95.

———. *This is Moscow Speaking and Other Stories.* New York: Collier Books, 1970.

Berdyaev, Nicolas. *The Origin of Russian Communism.* Translated by R. M. French. Ann Arbor: University of Michigan Press, 1960 [1937].

———. "Spirits of the Russian Revolution." http://www.berdyaev.com/berdiaev/berd_lib/1918_299.html.

———, et al. *Landmarks: A Collection of Essays on the Russian Intelligentsia, 1909.* Edited by Boris Shragin and Albert Todd. Translated by Marian Schwartz. New York: Karz Howard, 1977.

Berman, Ronald, ed. *Solzhenitsyn at Harvard*. Washington, DC: Ethics and Public Policy Center, 1980.

Bulgakov, Sergei. *Karl Marx as a Religious Type: His Relation to the Religion of Anthropotheism of L. Feuerbach*. Edited by Virgil R. Lang. Translated by Luba Barna. Belmont, MA: Nordland Publishing, 1979 [1907].

————. *The Orthodox Church*. Translation revised by Lydia Kesich. Crestwood, NY: St. Vladimir's Seminary Press, 1988.

Bunin, Ivan. *Cursed Days: A Diary of Revolution*. Translated and introduced by Thomas Gaiton Marullo. Chicago: Ivan R. Dee, 1998.

Burke, Edmund. *Reflections on the Revolution in France*. Edited by Conor Cruise O'Brien. New York: Penguin Books, 1968 [1790].

Chernyshevsky, Nikolai. *What Is to Be Done?* Translated by Michael R. Katz. Annotated by William G. Wagner. Ithaca, NY: Cornell University Press, 1989.

Dos Passos, John. *1919*. Volume 2 of U.S.A. Trilogy. Boston: Mariner Books, 2000.

Dostoyevsky, Fyodor. *The Devils*. Translated by David Magarshack. London: Penguin Books, 1971 [1953].

————. *The House of the Dead*. Translated by David McDuff. Harmondsworth: Penguin Books, 1985.

————. *Notes from Underground, White Nights, The Dream of a Ridiculous Man, and selections from The House of the Dead*. Translated by Andrew R. MacAndrew. New York: New American Library, 1961.

Fedotov, G. P., ed. *A Treasury of Russian Spirituality*. New York: Harper Torchbooks, 1965 [1950].

Gogol, Nikolai. *Selected Passages from Correspondence with Friends*. Translated by Jesse Zeldin. Nashville, TN: Vanderbilt University Press, 1969.

Grossman, Vasily. *Life and Fate*. Translated by Robert Chandler. New York: New York Review Books, 2006.

————. *A Writer at War: A Soviet Journalist with the Red Army, 1941–1945*. Edited and translated by Antony Beevor and Luba Vinogradova. New York: Vintage Books, 2007.

Hayward, Max, ed. *On Trial: The Soviet State versus "Abram Tertz" and "Nikolai Arzhak."* Translated by Max Hayward. New York: Harper and Row, 1967.

Herz, Martin F., ed. *Decline of the West? George Kennan and His Critics*. Washington, DC: Ethics and Public Policy Center, 1978.

Huxley, Aldous. *Brave New World*. New York: Harper and Row/Perennial Library, 1969 [1932, 1946].

Lenin, V. I. "Concerning *Vekhi*." http://www.marxists.org/archive/lenin/works/1909/dec/13.htm.

Likhachev, Dmitry S. *Reflections on the Russian Soul: A Memoir*. Translated by Bernard Adams. Translation edited by A. R. Tulloch. Budapest: Central European University Press, 2000.

Nechaev, Sergei [and Mikhail Bakunin]. "Catechism of a Revolutionist." http://pages.uoregon.edu/kimball/Nqv.catechism.thm.htm.

Orwell, George. *1984*. New York: Signet Classics, 1961 [1950].

Panin, Dimitri. *The Notebooks of Sologdin*. Translated by John Moore. New York: Harcourt Brace Jovanovich, 1976.

Pipes, Richard, ed. *The Unknown Lenin: From the Secret Archive*. Translated by Catherine A. Fitzpatrick. New Haven, CT: Yale University Press, 1998 [1996].

———. *Vixi: Memoirs of a Non-Belonger*. New Haven, CT: Yale University Press, 2003.

Putin, Vladimir. *First Person: An Astonishingly Frank Self-Portrait*. Translated by Catherine A. Fitzpatrick, with Nataliya Gevorkyan, Natalya Timakova, and Andrei Kolesnikov. New York: Public Affairs, 2000.

Raeff, Marc, ed. *Russian Intellectual History: An Anthology*. New York: Harcourt, Brace and World, 1966.

Reshetovskaya, Natalya A. *Sanya: My Life with Aleksandr Solzhenitsyn*. Translated by Elena Ivanoff. Indianapolis, IN: Bobbs-Merrill, 1975.

Sakharov, Andrei D. *Sakharov Speaks*. New York: Vintage Books, 1974.

Salinger, J. D. *Franny and Zooey*. New York: Back Bay Books, 2001 [1961].

Scammell, Michael, ed. *The Solzhenitsyn Files: Secret Soviet Documents Reveal One Man's Fight Against the Monolith*. Translated by Catherine A. Fitzpatrick et al. (under the supervision of Michael Scammell). Chicago: edition q, 1995.

Schmemann, Alexander. *The Historical Road of Eastern Orthodoxy*. Translated by Lydia W. Kesich. Crestwood, NY: St. Vladimir's Seminary Press, 2003.

———. *I Believe . . . : Celebration of Faith*. Vol. 1. Crestwood, NY: St. Vladimir's Seminary Press, 2003.

———. *The Journals of Father Alexander Schmemann 1973–1983*. Translated by Juliana Schmemann. Crestwood, NY: St. Vladimir's Seminary Press, 2002.

Schmemann, Juliana. *My Journey with Father Alexander*. Montreal: Alexander Press, 2006.

Shafarevich, Igor. *The Socialist Phenomenon*. Translated by William Tjalsma. Foreword by Aleksandr I. Solzhenitsyn. http://robert/stephens.com/essays/shafarevich/001SocialistPhenomenon.html.

Shalamov, Varlam. *Kolyma Tales*. Translated by John Glad. London: Penguin Books, 1994.

Solzhenitsyn, Natalia. "Returning to 'The GULag.'" Translated by Alexis Klimoff. Introduction by Daniel J. Mahoney. *New Criterion* 31, no. 1 (2012): 4–12.

Stoppard, Tom. *Travesties*. New York: Grove Press, 1975.

Tertz, Abram (Andrei Sinyavsky). *On Socialist Realism*. Translated by George Dennis. New York: Pantheon Books, 1960.

Tolstoy, Leo. "What Men Live By." In *Master and Man and Other Stories*. Translated by Ronald Wilks and Paul Foote, 143–66. London: Penguin Books, 2005.

Zhukov, Georgi K. *Marshal Zhukov's Greatest Battles*. Translated by Theodore Shabad. Edited by Harrison E. Salisbury. New York: Cooper Square Press, 2002.

SECONDARY SOURCES

Afanasiev, Victor. *Elder Barsanuphius of Optina*. Platina, CA: St. Herman of Alaska Brotherhood, 2000.

Applebaum, Anne. *GULag: A History*. New York: Anchor Books, 2004.

Ascher, Abraham. *P. A. Stolypin: The Search for Stability in Late Imperial Russia*. Stanford, CA: Stanford University Press, 2001.

Berlin, Isaiah. *Russian Thinkers*. Edited by Henry Hardy and Aileen Kelly. New York: Penguin Books, 1979.

Berlinski, David. *The Devil's Delusion: Atheism and Its Scientific Pretensions*. New York: Crown Forum, 2008.

Billington, James H. *The Icon and the Axe: An Interpretive History of Russian Culture.* New York: Vintage Books, 1970.

Bork, Robert H. *Slouching towards Gomorrah: Modern Liberalism and American Decline.* New York: Regan Books, 1996.

Bourdeaux, Michael. *Patriarch and Prophets: Persecution of the Russian Orthodox Church Today.* New York: Praeger, 1970.

Buchanan, Patrick J. *Suicide of a Superpower: Will America Survive to 2025?* New York: Thomas Dunne Books, 2011.

Burleigh, Michael. *Earthly Powers: The Clash of Religion and Politics in Europe, From the French Revolution to the Great War.* New York: Harper Perennial, 2007 [2005].

———. *Sacred Causes: The Clash of Religion and Politics, From the Great War to the War on Terror.* New York: Harper Perennial, 2008 [2006].

Chamberlain, Lesley. *Lenin's Private War: The Voyage of the Philosophy Steamer and the Exile of the Intelligentsia.* New York: Picador, 2008 [2006].

Chetverikov, Fr. Sergius. *Elder Ambrose of Optina.* Platina, CA: St. Herman of Alaska Brotherhood, 1997.

Clément, Olivier. *The Spirit of Solzhenitsyn.* Translated by Sarah Fawcett and Paul Burns. London: Search Press, 1976.

Congdon, Lee. "The Age of Newspeak." *Virginia Viewpoint,* no. 2002-11 (2002).

———. "Conservatism, Christianity, and the Revitalization of Europe." *Modern Age* 49, no. 4 (2007): 490-97.

———. "Culture War." *Virginia Viewpoint,* no. 2005-5 (2005).

———. *Exile and Social Thought: Hungarian Intellectuals in Germany and Austria, 1919-1933.* Princeton, NJ: Princeton University Press, 1991.

———. *George Kennan: A Writing Life.* Wilmington, DE: ISI Books, 2008.

———. "Lukács, Camus, and the Russian Terrorists." *Continuity,* no. 1 (1980): 17-36.

———. "Solzhenitsyn Wasn't Western." *American Conservative* 13, no. 5 (2014): 56-57.

Conquest, Robert. *The Great Terror: A Reassessment.* New York: Oxford University Press, 1990.

———. *Kolyma: The Arctic Death Camps.* New York: Viking, 1978.

Courtois, Stéphane, et al. *The Black Book of Communism: Crimes, Terror, Repression.* Translated by Jonathan Murphy and Mark Kramer. Cambridge, MA: Harvard University Press, 1999.

Cunningham, James W. *A Vanquished Hope: The Movement for Church Renewal in Russia, 1905-1906.* Crestwood, NY: St. Vladimir's Seminary Press, 1981.

Daly, Jonathan W. "'Storming the Last Citadel': The Bolshevik Assault on the Church, 1922." In *The Bolsheviks in Russian Society: The Revolution and the Civil Wars.* Edited by Vladimir N. Brovkin, 235-68. New Haven: Yale University Press, 1997.

Danilenko, Vladimir. "The Assassination of Pyotr Stolypin, 1911: A Collection of Documents." http://www.eastview.com/files/StolypinEngReview.pdf.

Davis, Nathaniel. *A Long Walk to Church: A Contemporary History of Russian Orthodoxy.* Boulder, CO: Westview Press, 1995.

Devlin, F. Roger. "Solzhenitsyn on the Jews and Tsarist Russia." http//toqonline.com/archives/V8n3/TOQv8n3Devlin.pdf.

Dunlop, John B., et al., eds. *Aleksandr Solzhenitsyn: Critical Essays and Documentary Materials.* 2nd ed. New York: Collier Books, 1975.

Epstein, Joseph. *A Literary Education and Other Essays*. Edinburg, VA: Axios Press, 2014.

Ericson, Edward E., Jr. "For the Love of Russia." *Modern Age* 42, no. 2 (2000): 205–9.

——, and Alexis Klimoff. *The Soul and Barbed Wire: An Introduction to Solzhenitsyn*. Wilmington, DE: ISI Books, 2008.

Fletcher, William C. *The Russian Orthodox Church Underground, 1917–1970*. London: Oxford University Press, 1971.

Frank, Joseph. *Dostoevsky: The Mantle of the Prophet, 1871–1881*. Princeton, NJ: Princeton University Press, 2002.

——. *Dostoevsky: The Miraculous Years, 1865–1871*. Princeton, NJ: Princeton University Press, 1995.

Garrard, John and Carol Garrard. *Russian Orthodoxy Resurgent: Faith and Power in the New Russia*. Princeton, NJ: Princeton University Press, 2008.

Gereben, Ágnes. "A bolsevik állam és az ortodox egyház: 1917–1920" ("The Bolshevik State and the Orthodox Church"). *Valóság* 44, no. 3 (2001): 71–91.

Gottlieb, Christian. *Dilemmas of Reaction in Leninist Russia: The Christian Response to the Revolution in the Works of N. A. Berdyaev, 1917–1924*. Odense: University Press of Southern Denmark, 2003.

Gray, J. Glenn. *The Warriors: Reflections on Men in Battle*. Lincoln: University of Nebraska Press, 1998 [1959].

Hamant, Yves. *Alexander Men: A Witness for Contemporary Russia (A Man For Our Times)*. Translated by Fr. Steven Bigham. Torrance, CA: Oakwood Publications, 1995.

Hart, David Bentley. *Atheist Delusions: The Christian Revolution and Its Fashionable Enemies*. New Haven, CT: Yale University Press, 2009.

——. *The Doors of the Sea: Where Was God in the Tsunami?* Grand Rapids, MI: William B. Eerdmans, 2005.

Hollander, Paul. *The End of Commitment: Intellectuals, Revolutionaries, and Political Morality*. Chicago: Ivan R. Dee, 2006.

Husband, William B. *"Godless Communists": Atheism and Society in Soviet Russia, 1917–1932*. DeKalb: Northern Illinois University Press, 2000.

Kavelin, Fr. Leonid. *Elder Macarius of Optina*. Platina, CA: St. Herman of Alaska Brotherhood, 1995.

Kizenko, Nadieszda. *A Prodigal Saint: Father John of Kronstadt and the Russian People*. University Park, PA: Pennsylvania State University Press, 2000.

Kline, George L. *Religious and Anti-Religious Thought in Russia*. Chicago: University of Chicago Press, 1968.

Kolakowski, Leszek. *Is God Happy? Selected Essays*. New York: Basic Books, 2013.

Kun, Miklós. *Stalin: An Unknown Portrait*. Translated by Miklós Bodóczky, Rachel Hideg, János Hideg, and Miklós Vörös. Budapest: Central European University Press, 2003.

Larson, Nathan D. *Aleksandr Solzhenitsyn and the Modern Russo-Jewish Question*. Stuttgart: Ibidem-Verlag, 1005.

Legutko, Ryszard. *The Demon in Democracy: Totalitarian Temptations in Free Societies*. Translated by Teresa Adelson. New York: Encounter Books, 2016.

Leong, Albert, ed. *The Millennium: Christianity and Russia (A.D. 988–1988)*. Crestwood, NY: St. Vladimir's Seminary Press, 1990.

Lincoln, W. Bruce. *Between Heaven and Hell: The Story of a Thousand Years of Artistic Life in Russia*. New York: Viking, 1998.

————. *The Conquest of a Continent: Siberia and the Russians*. New York: Random House, 1994.

————. *The Great Reforms: Autocracy, Bureaucracy, and the Politics of Change in Imperial Russia*. DeKalb: Northern Illinois University Press, 1990.

————. *In War's Dark Shadow: The Russians before the Great War*. New York: Dial Press, 1983.

————. *Passage through Armageddon: The Russians in War and Revolution, 1914–1918*. New York: Simon and Schuster, 1986.

————. *Red Victory: A History of the Russian Civil War*. New York: Simon and Schuster, 1989.

Lynch, Allen C. *Vladimir Putin and Russian Statecraft*. Washington, DC: Potomac Books, 2011.

Mahoney, Daniel J. *Aleksandr Solzhenitsyn: The Ascent from Ideology*. Lanham, MD: Rowman and Littlefield, 2001.

————. *The Other Solzhenitsyn: Telling the Truth about a Misunderstood Writer and Thinker*. South Bend, IN: St. Augustine's Press, 2014.

————. "The Wheel Turns." http://www.newcriterion.com/articles.cfm/wheelturns-mahoney.

Malia, Martin. *The Soviet Tragedy: A History of Socialism in Russia, 1917–1991*. New York: Free Press, 1994.

Montefiore, Simon Sebag. *Stalin: The Court of the Red Tsar*. New York: Vintage Books, 2005 [2003].

————. *Young Stalin*. New York: Vintage Books, 2008.

Nielsen, Niels C., Jr. *Solzhenitsyn's Religion*. Nashville, TN: Thomas Nelson, 1975.

Overy, Richard. *Russia's War: A History of the Soviet War Effort: 1941–1945*. New York: Penguin Books, 1998.

Pearce, Joseph. *Solzhenitsyn: A Soul in Exile*. Grand Rapids, MI: Baker Books, 2001 [1999].

Pipes, Richard. *Struve: Liberal on the Right, 1905–1944*. Cambridge: Harvard University Press, 1980.

Pospielovsky, Dimitry. *The Russian Church under the Soviet Regime, 1917–1982*, I–II. Crestwood, NY: St. Vladimir's Seminary Press, 1984.

Pyman, Avril. *Pavel Florensky: A Quiet Genius: The Tragic and Extraordinary Life of Russia's Unknown da Vinci*. New York: Continuum, 2010.

Raeff, Marc. "Enticements and Rifts: Georges Florovsky as Russian Intellectual Historian." In *Georges Florovsky: Russian Intellectual and Orthodox Churchman*. Edited by Andrew Blane, 219–86. Crestwood, NY: St. Vladimir's Seminary Press, 1993.

————. *Russia Abroad: A Cultural History of the Russian Emigration, 1919–1939*. New York: Oxford University Press, 1990.

Robinson, Paul. "Putin's Philosophy." *American Conservative*. http://www .theamericanconservative.com/blog/putins-philosophy.

Robson, Roy R. *Old Believers in Modern Russia*. DeKalb: Northern Illinois University Press, 1995.

————. *Solovki: The Story of Russia Told through Its Most Remarkable Islands*. New Haven, CT: Yale University Press, 2004.

Scammell, Michael. *Solzhenitsyn: A Biography*. New York: W. W. Norton, 1984.

Schapiro, Leonard. *Russian Studies*. Edited by Ellen Dahrendorf. Introduction by Harry Willetts. New York: Viking, 1987.

Slezkine, Yuri. *The Jewish Century*. Princeton, NJ: Princeton University Press, 2004.

Stanton, Leonard J., and James D. Hardy, Jr. *Interpreting Nikolai Gogol within Russian Orthodoxy: A Neglected Influence on the First Great Russian Novelist*. Lewiston, NY: Edwin Mellen Press, 2006.

Steyn, Mark. *After America: Get Ready for Armageddon*. Washington, DC: Regnery Publishing, 2011.

Struve, Nikita. *Christians in Contemporary Russia*. Translated by Lancelot Sheppard and A. Manson. New York: Charles Scribner's Sons, 1967.

Szamuely, Tibor. *The Russian Tradition*. London: Fontana Press, 1988 [1974].

Thomas, D. M. *Alexander Solzhenitsyn: A Century in His Life*. New York: St. Martin's Press, 1998.

Tolczyk, Dariusz. *See No Evil: Literary Cover-Ups and Discoveries of the Soviet Camp Experience*. New Haven, CT: Yale University Press, 1999.

Treisman, Daniel. *The Return: Russia's Journey from Gorbachev to Medvedev*. New York: Free Press, 2011.

Turner, Henry Ashby, Jr. *Hitler's Thirty Days to Power*. Reading, MA: Addison-Wesley, 1996.

Volkogonov, Dmitri. *Autopsy for an Empire: The Seven Leaders Who Built the Soviet Regime*. Translated and edited by Harold Shukman. New York: Free Press, 1998.

——. *Lenin: A New Biography*. Translated and edited by Harold Shukman. New York: Free Press, 1994.

Ware, Timothy. *The Orthodox Church*. London: Penguin Books, 1993.

Werth, Nicolas. "A State against Its People: Violence, Repression, and Terror in the Soviet Union." In *The Black Book of Communism: Crimes, Terror, Repression*, by Stéphane Courtois et al. Translated by Jonathan Murphy and Mark Kramer. Cambridge, MA: Harvard University Press, 1999.

Wilson, Elizabeth. *Rostropovich: The Musical Life of the Great Cellist, Teacher, and Legend*. Chicago: Ivan R. Dee, 2008.

Yakolev, Alexander N. *A Century of Violence in Soviet Russia*. Translated by Anthony Austin. Foreword by Paul Hollander. New Haven, CT: Yale University Press, 2002.

Yazykova, Irina. *Hidden and Triumphant: The Underground Struggle to Save Russian Iconography*. Translated by Paul Grenier. Brewster, MA: Paraclete Press, 2010.

Zernov, Nicolas. *The Russian Religious Renaissance of the Twentieth Century*. New York: Harper and Row, 1963.

Zubok, Vladislav. *Zhivago's Children: The Last Russian Intelligentsia*. Cambridge, MA: Belknap Press of Harvard University Press, 2009.

INDEX

Lightning Source UK Ltd.
Milton Keynes UK
UKHW010159200320
360652UK00005B/377